Behavior
Modification

ISSUES and EXTENSIONS

Contributors

Felipe Acosta N.

Teodore Ayllon

Sidney W. Bijou

Rodolpho Carbonari Sant'Anna

Dementrio Carmona

Harold L. Cohen

Benjamin Dominguez T.

C. B. Ferster

Dean L. Fixsen

Florente Lopez R.

K. Daniel O'Leary

Jorge Peralta

Elery L. Phillips

Emilio Ribes-Inesta

B. F. Skinner

Robert G. Wahler

Montrose M. Wolf

Patricia Wright

Behavior Modification

ISSUES and EXTENSIONS

Edited by

SIDNEY W. BIJOU
University of Illinois at Champaign-Urbana
Champaign, Illinois

EMILIO RIBES-INESTA
National Autonomous University of Mexico
Mexico City, Mexico

ACADEMIC PRESS   New York and London   1972

ACADEMIC PRESS, INC.
111 Fifth Avenue, New York, New York 10003

United Kingdom Edition published by
ACADEMIC PRESS, INC. (LONDON) LTD.
24/28 Oval Road. London NW1

LIBRARY OF CONGRESS CATALOG CARD NUMBER: 79-187256

PRINTED IN THE UNITED STATES OF AMERICA

Contents

SOME RELATIONS BETWEEN BEHAVIOR MODIFICATION AND BASIC RESEARCH
B. F. Skinner

SOME ECOLOGICAL PROBLEMS IN CHILD BEHAVIOR MODIFICATION
Robert G. Wahler

251674

NEW ROLES FOR THE PARAPROFESSIONAL

Teodoro Ayllon and Patricia Wright

DISCUSSION: A NEW PERSPECTIVE: CHRONIC PATIENTS AS ASSISTANTS IN A BEHAVIOR REHABILITATION PROGRAM IN A PSYCHIATRIC INSTITUTION

Benjamin Dominguez T., Felipe Acosta N., and Dementrio Carmona

AN EXPERIMENTAL ANALYSIS OF CLINICAL PHENOMENA

C. B. Ferster

List of Contributors

Numbers in parentheses indicate the pages on which the authors' contributions begin.

FELIPE ACOSTA N. (127), National Autonomous University of Mexico, Mexico City, Mexico

TEODORE AYLLON (115), Georgia State University, Atlanta, Georgia

SIDNEY W. BIJOU (27), University of Illinois at Champaign-Urbana, Champaign, Illinois

RODOLPHO CARBONARI SANT'ANNA (109), Autonomous University of Santo Domingo, Santo Domingo, Dominican Republic

DEMENTRIO CARMONA (127), National Autonomous University of Mexico, Mexico City, Mexico

HAROLD L. COHEN (63), Institute for Behavioral Research, Silver Springs, Maryland

BENJAMIN DOMINGUEZ T.,* (127), National Autonomous University of Mexico, Mexico City, Mexico

C. B. FERSTER (133), The American University, Washington, D.C.

*Present address: Departamento de Psiocologia, Carcel Preventive de "Villa Obregón," Mexico, D.F.

DEAN L. FIXSEN (51), Department of Human Development, University of Kansas, Lawrence, Kansas

FLORENTE LOPEZ R., (43), University of Veracruz, Xalapa, Mexico

K. DANIEL O'LEARY (93), Psychology Department, State University of New York, Stony Brook, New York

JORGE PERALTA (19), University of Veracruz, Xalapa, Mexico

ELERY L. PHILLIPS (51), University of Kansas, Lawrence, Kansas

EMILIO RIBES-INESTA (85), National Autonomous University of Mexico, Mexico City, Mexico

B. F. SKINNER (1), Harvard University, Cambridge, Massachusetts

ROBERT G. WAHLER (7), Psychology Department, University of Tennessee, Knoxville, Tennessee

MONTROSE M. WOLF (51), Department of Human Development, University of Kansas, Laurence, Kansas

PATRICIA WRIGHT (115), Georgia State University, Atlanta, Georgia

Preface

The papers in this volume were delivered at the First Annual Symposium on Behavior Modification held at the University of Veracruz, Xalapa, Mexico, January, 1971. They vary in the emphasis given to the theoretical and practical aspects of the problem. The first paper by Skinner and the last by Ferster are devoted entirely to theoretical issues, whereas most of the others deal with theoretical matters only as they relate to a particular area of behavioral technology. The order of papers on some phase of behavioral technology is roughly genetic, with Wahler and Peralta focusing on young children and child-rearing practices, and Ayllon and Wright, and Dominguez, Acosta, and Carmona on behavioral techniques for institutionalized psychotic adults. Several of the papers discuss the training of paraprofessional personnel. Participants in the Symposium were asked to consider this problem, insofar as they could, because it is of prime interest to psychologists in Mexico, Central America, and South America. It is the consensus among Latin American psychologists, first, that the application of behavior modification techniques to education, psychotherapy, and rehabilitation cannot help but ameliorate the existing problems in those fields, and, second, that widespread use of these techniques in the near future will depend on their resources for training a large number of nonprofessionals. While the primary papers are authored by psychologists from the United States, the discussant papers are by psychologists from Mexico and the Dominican Republic, each of whom related the material in the primary paper to situations as they exist mainly in his own country.

   The Symposium is a milestone in the rapidly growing interest in behavior modification in Mexico and other Latin American countries. In 1964, a group of young Mexican psychologists at the University of Veracruz, Xalapa, began to introduce behavioral approaches in their teaching, research, and community services. Their efforts were supplemented mainly through the efforts of Professor Emilio Ribes-Inesta who arranged consultations, colloquia, and seminars by American psychologists. An account of psychology in Mexico during this period appeared in 1968 in the *American Psychologist* **23**, number 8. In response to requests for information about and training in behavior principles and behavior modification from students and young faculty in other parts of Mexico and from several South American countries, Professor Ribes-Inesta organized the First Symposium on Behavior Modification. That the conference was well received is attested to by the attendance and enthusiasm. About 1000 were in attendance, and animated discussions, in and outside the conference hall, went on throughout the two days. A kind of *fiesta* prevailed.

   All of the authors prepared papers or revisions of papers especially for this volume. We are indebted to them for their promptness in submitting manscripts and for their indulgence in making changes required by the publisher. We wish to thank Professor Alcaraz, Dean of Sciences, for his general support in developing the psychology program, and the officials of the University of Veracruz for providing the facilities for the conference. We wish also to thank Janet R. Bijou and Barbara Grimm for their editorial work on the discussants' manuscripts, and to express our gratitude to Dorothy Whalen for typing the manuscripts and to Michael Whalen for assisting in the preparation of the figures.

Sidney W. Bijou
Emilio Ribes-Inesta

Some Relations between Behavior Modification and Basic Research[1],[1a]

B. F. SKINNER

The first scientific laws were probably the rules of craftsmen. In other words, science seems to have emerged from efforts to solve practical problems. There are examples of this in psychology. Binet's invention of a way to place children in schools led to intelligence testing, and the problem of selecting personnel in industry led to other measures in what later became the psychology of individual differences. Clinical problems led Freud to invent the mental apparatus of psychoanalytic theory. Even the physiological psychology of Fechner and Wundt arose from efforts to solve certain philosophical problems concerning the nature of knowledge and the relation between mind and body. As science advances, however, the direction changes. Subject matters become too complex to yield to lay wisdom or rules of thumb, and it is the scientist who sees the useful implications of his discoveries. Most improvements in technology now come from what is essentially basic research. Behavior modification is an example. Its origins lay in a relatively "pure" experimental analysis.

The shaping of behavior through a step-by-step approximation to a final topography is a case in point. As a distinction began to be made between

[1]Preparation supported by Grant K6-MH-21, 775-01, National Institutes of Mental Health.

operant and respondent conditioning, or between emitted and elicited behavior, the role of the controlling stimulus changed, and problems arose. The experimenter had no control over the first instance of an operant response; he could only wait for it to appear. It seemed to follow that complex forms of behavior, which seldom if ever occurred, were essentially out of reach of operant conditioning. But the possibility remained that the component parts of a complex pattern might occur separately and that larger patterns might be constructed bit by bit.

An early effort to shape complex behavior was suggested by an experiment in which a chimpanzee used poker chips to operate a sort of vending machine (Cowles, 1927). It was implied by some writers that in doing so the chimpanzee demonstrated certain higher mental processes—in which, for example, the poker chip served a symbolic function. To show that operant conditioning could explain the behavior, I conditioned a rat to behave in a similar way. As originally reported in *The Behavior of Organisms* (Skinner, 1938), "every step in the process had to be worked out through a series of approximations, since the component responses were not in the original repertoire of the rat." Following the practice in early experiments on operant conditioning, and in other experiments on learning at that time, I made reinforcers contingent on behavior by constructing mechanical systems. To begin with, a number of marbles were strewn on the floor of the rat's cage. The sides of the cage were clear of the floor so that a marble could roll off any edge. Whenever a marble dropped off the floor, it tripped a switch and operated a food dispenser. When responses that caused marbles to roll about the floor became more frequent, three edges of the floor were blocked so that a marble could fall off only one edge, and movements that caused marbles to move in other directions underwent extinction. Later, only a small section of one edge was left clear, and the edge was then slightly raised. By this time the rat was pushing the marbles with its forepaws or nose and a strong directed response would force a marble up and over the edge and would be reinforced. Eventually the rat grasped and lifted the marble over the edge.

A new problem then arose. Evidently it is hard for a rat to acquire the operant of "letting go." It lets go of an object when it is either punished or not reinforced for holding on, but apparently it learns only with difficulty to do so "to produce an effect." The rat would hold the marble over the edge, showing a considerable tremor because of the unnatural posture, and eventually the marble would fall from its paws. (At one stage, it learned to knock the marble out of its paws with its nose, often shooting it some distance, and a sort of backstop had to be built to make sure the marble would not miss the triggering platform below.) Eventually an appropriate response of letting go appeared.

The edge and the backstop were then changed to form a slot, which grew smaller in cross section and taller until it was eventually a tube less than one inch in diameter extending two inches above the floor A rack was then added from which a marble could be obtained by pulling a chain that hung from the top of the cage. In the final performance the rat would pull the chain, pick up the marble thus discharged, walk on its hind legs across the cage, lift the marble tremblingly to the top of the tube, and drop it in.

The curious thing about this experiment, seen in retrospect, is that every step in the shaping process was taken by *changing the equipment.* Mechanical contingencies have the advantage that they work in the absence of the experimenter, and in spite of much evidence to the contrary I may have been under the influence of early learning theories in which it was assumed that a great many trials were needed to teach a rat anything. [I made the same mistake with my students; I assumed that they would always need to go over material more than once, and the first teaching machine designed for their use allowed for the presentation of each item until two correct responses had been made (Skinner, 1968).]

I well remember the day when Norman Guttman, Keller Breland, and I discovered how wrong all this was by dispensing with mechanical contingencies and reinforcing successive approximations to a complex response by hand. By operating a food dispenser with a hand switch we taught a pigeon to strike a wooden ball with a swiping motion of its beak and to knock the ball about its cage, rather in the manner of a squash player. Shaping complex behavior through a programmed sequence of contingencies is now so commonplace that it is hard to understand why we should have been amazed at the speed with which this was done.

Another useful principle discovered in basic research has to do with the maintenance of behavior. Early experiments on learning concentrated on certain conspicuous facts—the acquisition of new forms of behavior (in learning) and the disappearance of old ones (in forgetting). "Overlearning" was studied, but there was no recognition of the fact that behavior could be maintained in various states of strength by appropriate schedules of reinforcement. Schedules are now widely used to solve what are essentially practical problems—for example, in generating baselines to show drug effects and emotional changes such as the conditioned suppression called "anxiety," but the implications for behavior modification have not been fully explored. Although the maintenance of available behavior in strength through intermittent reinforcement is an important practical problem, the emphasis is still on the production of new behavior. But this will change as practical implications are discovered. The behavior modification of the future will also make a far more extensive use of the control exerted by the current environment, of deprivation and satiation, of the conditioning of new reinforcers, and of the explicit design of instructional repertoires (of which imitation is an example).

Not all innovations in behavior modification are traceable to a basic analysis, of course, and traditional rules of thumb for shaping and maintaining behavior that use the same principles arose long before any research had been done. The analysis is nevertheless important in interpreting and explaining the effect of a method, whatever its provenance. It is hard to see the contingencies of reinforcement that prevail in daily life and hence to understand the behavior they generate (Skinner, 1969). Laboratory research tells us what to look for and, equally important, what to ignore, and in doing so it leads to the improvement of practical contingencies.

It is not always easy to maintain a distinction between basic and applied research, since both may use the same methods and equipment and come up with the same kinds of results, but an important difference lies in the reasons why research is undertaken and supported. The applied researcher is under the influence of a special kind of consequence. He carries on, in part, because he will make someone healthier or wealthier rather than simply wiser. This is not a reflection on his "purity" or any other trait of character. It is simply a fact that bears on certain characteristics of his practice, and for that reason some further relations between applied and basic research are worth considering.

One obvious value of practical results is illustrated by the history of the experimental analysis of behavior. Operant research was not at first generously supported by departments of psychology, and many young researchers took jobs in laboratories—in pharmaceutical companies, for example—which were supported because of practical consequences. It was not always necessary to design research under the influence of such consequences, however, and many important basic experiments were carried out. Even when the practical consequences were stressed, there was often a gain in basic knowledge.

Behavior modification supplies another example. Its practical implications have led to the support of work from which contributions to basic knowledge are being made. Practical consequences often force the scientist to deal with variables he would otherwise put off for later consideration. To improve the lives of institutionalized retardates or psychotics, for example, it is usually necessary to deal with more variables than convenience dictates, and the simplifying practices of the laboratory are not feasible. As a result, discoveries are made that standard experimental practice would, in a sense, put out of reach.

A contribution in the other direction—from basic to applied—would traditionally be described as the "confidence" with which contingencies are now designed in solving practical problems. Laboratory successes generalize to daily life. The effects of reinforcement are often deferred and need to be mediated, and this is particularly true when reinforcement is used in place of punishment, because the latter has quicker effects. The amenable conditions of the laboratory are likely to bring the researcher under the control of deferred consequences and to maintain his behavior when it is only intermittently reinforced. A practical method may continue to be used because of its success, but help from basic research is often needed in its early development. Techniques of behavior modification often seem, after the fact, like the plainest of common sense, but we should remember that they remained undiscovered or unused for a long time and that the same "common sense" still leads to many violations of the basic principles.

The theory that accompanies an experimental analysis is particularly helpful in justifying practice, because behavior modification often means a vast change in the way in which we deal with people. It is vast not only in scope (touching fields as diverse as education, psychotherapy, economics, and government) but in its very nature, as the states of mind, feelings, and other attributes of the inner man who figures in traditional explanations of human behavior are rejected in favor of antecedent circumstances in a person's genetic and individual histories. The genetic history is at the moment beyond control, but the environmental history, past and present, can be supplemented and changed, and that is what is done in a genuine technology of behavior. Behavior modification is environment modification, but this is not widely recognized. Very little current "behavioral science" is really behavioral, because prescientific modes of explanation still flourish, but behavior modification is an outstanding exception.

One practical contribution of an experimental analysis is easily overlooked. It is derived from the scientific methodology upon which the analysis is based. Applied psychologists have usually found themselves in a subordinate position. They have served as fact finders rather than decision makers. More than any other science, psychology has had to move against a weight of folklore, superstition, and error, and it is not surprising that psychologists have put a premium on the factual and objective. They have struggled to escape from the limitations of personal experience. To know what a man actually hears or sees they have controlled the stimulating environment. To know what he does or says they have recorded his behavior as precisely as possible and quantified it with inventories, questionnaires, and tests. To discover what he is inclined to do or say they have sampled his opinions and beliefs.

This "objectivity" has no doubt been valuable, but it has cast the psychologist in a merely supportive role. Clinical psychologists and psychometricians find themselves testing patients and supplying the information to the psychiatrist who carries on with therapy. The school psychologist reports to a teacher or administrator, who is the one who takes appropriate action. The results of opinion polls are used by statesmen or politicians, not by the pollsters, and it is the directors who plan the future of a company in the light of a market analysis. When a psychologist moves into a decision-making spot, it is generally felt that he is no longer acting as a psychologist. Something of the same sort holds for all the behavioral sciences, and the relationship has, in fact, been given semi-official status. An "Advisory Committee on Government Programs in the Behavioral Sciences," appointed by the National Academy of Sciences and the National Research Council in 1965,[2] has been careful to point out that "there is no assumption . . . that knowledge is a substitute for wisdom or common sense or for decision-making."

The wisdom, common sense, or decision-making faculty thus denied to social scientists is probably a remnant of a prescientific autonomous man. It is not supported by the conception of human behavior that emerges from an experimental analysis, and this fact explains the unique characteristic of behavior modification that it *is* directly concerned with decision making and control. When we have specified the goals to which "wisdom and common sense" are to

---

[2] Quoted in a review by Albert D. Biderman (*Science, 1970,* 169, 1064-1067) of the report of the Young Committee, appointed by NAS-NRC in 1965 as "Advisory Committee on Government Programs in the Behavior Sciences" *Politics of Social Research* by Ralph L. Beals, Aldine, Chicago, 1969.

be applied, we may go straight to the design of relevant contingencies. The experimental analysis of behavior is more than measurement. It is more than testing hypotheses. It is an empirical attack upon the manipulable variables of which behavior is a function. As a result the behavior modifier plays an exceptional role.

Even so, he may find it difficult to move into a position where important decisions are made. Changes in practice do not usually come about in the center of power. It is not the administrator or teacher who is likely to make a major contribution to instruction, but rather those who analyze teaching and learning experimentally. It is not the employer or worker who is likely to propose better incentive systems but rather someone who has examined the effects of reinforcers on human behavior in general. We have become used to this fact in medicine, where major improvements come from sciences peripheral to medicine itself rather than from practicing physicians. But unlike the physician, who has learned to accept new practices originating elsewhere, the administrator, teacher, psychiatrist, or industrialist may feel that he has a special kind of wisdom arising from familiarity with his field and may resist the application of a basic science or a new method closely associated with such a science. The current condition of American elementary and high school education is a tragic example. Prevailing practices are derived from unscientific "philosophies of education" and from the personal experiences of administrators and teachers, and the results are particularly disturbing to those who know what might be done instead. The first behavior that needs to be modified is obviously that of the teacher, administrator, or philosopher of education.

Another practical consequence of basic research remains to be emphasized. Our culture has made us all sensitive to the good of others, and we are generously reinforced when we act for their good, but the display of gratitude that reinforces the teacher or therapist who is in immediate contact with another person is often dangerous. Those who are especially sensitive to the good of others are often induced to go into teaching or therapy rather than basic research. Progress would be more rapid if the same kind of reinforcement could be brought to bear on the researcher, if he could be appropriately affected by the extraordinary extent to which he is also acting for the good of others. The basic researcher has, in fact, a tremendous advantage. Any slight advance in our understanding of human behavior that leads to improved practices in behavior modification will eventually work for the good of *billions* of people.

REFERENCES

Cowles, J. T., Food tokens as incentives for learning by chimpanzees. *Comp. Psychol. Monograph,* 1937, 14(5).
Skinner, B. F. *Behavior of organisms.* New York: Appleton, 1938.
Skinner, B. F. *The technology of teaching.* New York: Appleton, 1968. p. 36, Fig. 4.
Skinner, B. F. *Contingencies of reinforcement: a theoretical analysis.* New York: Appleton, 1969.

Some Ecological Problems
in Child Behavior Modification

ROBERT G. WAHLER

The assumptions of reinforcement theory are by now familiar to many, particularly to those who deal clinically with children. It is argued that children behave as they do because of the payoff or reinforcement such behaviors obtain from the child's environment. Children adopt those behaviors that are maximally effective in producing social stimulation from parents, peers, teachers, and other members of their immediate communities. Thus, if members of the community consider the child to be deviant because of what he does or does not do, the problem should have a rather straightforward solution. First, one discovers how the deviant behavior obtains reinforcement from the social environment. In so doing, one should also find answers to why the child's more desirable behavior is not occurring. For example, direct observation should reveal that the aggressive child receives reliable attention following his assertive behavior, but perhaps not following his more passive actions. The retarded child may be seen to acquire frequent attention from concerned adults following self head-banging and face-slapping; yet, his quiet play may be ignored by the same adults. While the school-phobic child may obtain immediate teacher and peer reactions by crying, his reading and writing may receive none.

It stands to reason that if social attention is a reliable and reinforcing consequence of the child's deviant behavior, a systematic shift in these social contingencies should be therapeutic. If members of the child's immediate community could be trained to ignore his deviant behavior and respond instead to his more normal behavior, his normal behaviors should become characteristic features; his deviant behaviors, since they are no longer reinforced, should cease to occur.

A DECEPTIVE SIMPLICITY

As the above two-step procedure indicates, assessment and treatment of deviant children are guided by a simple paradigm. Deviant behavior occurs because it is supported by reinforcement contingencies set by the child's social environment. Through observation, these contingencies should become apparent. Therapy then becomes a matter of shifting the contingencies such that members of the child's community become selectively attentive to his nondeviant behavior.

Now, while research support for these procedures is mounting rapidly (e.g., see Bandura, 1968), the clinician should not be misled by the apparent simplicity of assessment and treatment. True, the reinforcement model is simple to grasp. Unfortunately, its application to the child's real world is a good deal more complex and, thus, fraught with problems for the behavior modifier.

The complexity of child behavior in natural settings is vividly illustrated by "psychological ecologists" such as Barker (1965) and Barker and Wright (1955). These investigators pointed to a wide variety of behaviors that characterize a typical child; in addition, they described a vast multitude of interactions between the behaviors and social events produced by peers, parents, and other adults in the child's community. Whereas it would not be possible to portray the extensive nature of such interactions in this paper, the author's observational description of a parent and her child is instructive:

> Jimmy is standing on the couch in his living room. He is humming a tune and making circular motions on the wall with his hand. Jimmy's mother enters the room, looks at Jimmy and says: "Jimmy, stop messing up the wall and get off that couch!" Jimmy looks at his mother, stops touching the wall, and begins to jump up and down on the couch. Mother walks toward Jimmy and says: "I said get off the couch." Jimmy falls face forward on the couch just as mother reaches the couch. He turns on his back, looks at mother and says: "This is my couch too, you know." Mother sits on the couch beside Jimmy and touches his knee with her hand. She says softly: "Of course it's your couch. It belongs to the entire family." Jimmy stands beside the couch and speaks in a quavering voice: "Then I should be able to get on it whenever I want to. Sally does." Mother reaches for Jimmy's arm, grabs him, and pulls him toward her. He begins to cry and mother puts her arm around him. She says: "Why do you always have to cry over such little things?"

If one could extrapolate from this three-minute segment of the child's day at home, it immediately becomes apparent that a child's social interactions do not occur in easily defined stimulus-response units. In the above example, the behavior modifier would wish to conceptualize the mother's responses as possible reinforcing and discriminative stimuli for her child's various actions. On an abstract level this exercise would pose few problems. However, to do so in terms of concrete operations is another matter. One is not only faced with the task of measuring and later demonstrating relationships between the events of interest (in this case mother-child behaviors), but also with the practical problem of clinical intervention. That is, assuming that this child's behavior is deviant in some respect, what tactics can be employed in its modification? Fortunately, technological advancements have led to the solution of some of these problems; others have yet to be solved. In the author's experience, many of these problems fall under four main categories: stimulus settings for deviant behavior; the assessment of deviant behavior; treatment tactics for deviant behavior; and the generalization of treatment effects. The following sections of this paper are designed to explore some of these ecological problems, including attempts at their solution.

STIMULUS SETTINGS FOR DEVIANT BEHAVIOR

Deviant children commonly display their problem behaviors in a variety of environments. A child referred for treatment because of unusual behavior may produce this kind of behavior in his home and school classroom but perhaps not in his playground or on the streets of his city. This variable setting quality of deviant behavior may also be seen within specific environments. For example, the "negativistic" child may be negativistic at bedtime and at mealtime, but he may be quite cooperative at other times of his day at home. The same child at school may be considered difficult to manage during the arithmetic lesson but no problem during the social studies lesson. In other words, home and school environments can be broken into smaller units such as "when company comes," "breakfast," "recess," "nap time," "toilet time," etc. These units or stimulus settings are established functionally by the clinician in terms of the likelihood that they set the occasion for the child's deviant behavior.

As predicted by reinforcement theory (Bijou & Baer, 1961), child behavior is an important function of its immediate environmental contingencies. Thus, if the child's environment varies from time to time, his behavior should also vary. To follow up this assumption with an example, consider the negativistic child again. It is unlikely that his parents would provide supporting social contingencies for his negativistic behavior on a continual basis. They might do so in their attempts to get him to eat his meals or in their attempts to put him to bed. But, they may use completely different, and more successful, tactics in getting him to feed the family pet or mow the lawn. Thus, children are quite competent discriminators of social contingencies: much of their behavior appears appropriate to the variable pattern of social cues and consequences presented within and across their environments.

Recognition of setting variations within specific environments leads to the solution of two important technical problems in behavior modification. First, the most apparent problem concerns observation of the deviant child. Second, therapeutic training of important social attention dispensers in the child's environment is facilitated by this knowledge.

Workers in the child behavior therapy area have typically emphasized direct observation as an indispensable part of assessment (see Bijou, Peterson, & Ault, 1968). Observers, ranging from indigenous community members (Wahler & Erikson, 1969) to the child himself (Lovitt & Curtis, 1969), have been utilized to obtain such data. However, before any observational system can be implemented, the observers must be told what to observe and where to observe it. In view of the preceding description of setting variations, such instruction is not a simple matter of "observing in the child's home or school." Settings within these environments should be specified in terms of the likelihood that they may set the occasion for the child's deviant actions—if for no other reason than practical use of observer time. Preliminary work by Wahler and Cormier (1970) indicates that systematic interviewing of parents and teachers can produce this kind of information. These investigators developed an interview checklist offering specific guidelines to the interviewer's efforts in conducting setting analyses of home and school environments. Such information provides a valuable first step in implementing behavior modification programs in natural environments. Whereas parent and teacher reports on setting events are not always reliable, at least observers are equipped with guidelines on where to begin their observations.

Observational information on setting variations offers useful guidelines in training the deviant child's parents, teachers, and peers to operate as behavior modifiers. If the child's deviant actions occur in multiple settings within a specific environment, the clinician has the option of beginning the training program in any one of these settings. Parents and teachers often complain about the beginning difficulties of recording child behavior and responding selectively to it in some settings. For example, a teacher may find it extremely difficult to monitor "out-of-seat behavior" during the arithmetic lesson, at least in the beginning phases of her training. However, she might find it to be a simple matter during the silent reading period, assuming that this period also sets the occasion for out-of-seat behavior. Thus, in beginning training, the clinician would do well to choose that setting presenting the fewest training problems. As the "therapist" becomes competent in observing and responding to the child, the therapeutic program may then be shifted to more complex settings.

THE ASSESSMENT OF DEVIANT BEHAVIOR

Typical behavior therapy tactics would dictate not only weakening the child's deviant behavior but also strengthening an alternate class of desirable behavior. That is, a parent may be instructed to ignore her child's shouting *and* to attend systematically to his quiet talk. These tactics are based on the hope that strengthening the desirable class will suppress the deviant class, assuming, that is, that the desirable class is incompatible with the deviant member. In most cases, identifying an incompatible class of behavior is a relatively simple task. When the deviant class is established, its counterpart is often established by inference. Thus, the desirable counterpart of hitting might be cooperative play; clinging to mother might be replaced by play with other children.

With these treatment tactics in mind, the assessment phase of behavior modification should include observation of desirable as well as deviant aspects of child behavior. Usual practice first requires grouping the child's various behaviors on the basis of physical similarities. Thus, hitting, pinching, kicking, and biting might be considered as a single class of behavior; quiet solitary play and quiet play with peers could be defined as components of another response class. A similar categorizing of stimulus events provided by the child's social environment might also be conducted—although, typically, these events are considered collectively as larger classes—namely, parent social attention, peer social attention, etc.

Once the response and stimulus classes have been defined, observers are then told to count these events, paying particular attention to close temporal relationships between the response and stimulus categories. This done, one would expect a diagnostic picture made up of the comparative frequencies of desirable and deviant behaviors and stimuli responsible for their occurrence. According to one prediction from the reinforcement model, the greatest proportion of adult and peer social attention would be found to occur following the deviant behavior. Such a finding would lead one to speculate that the deviant behavior occurs more frequently than its desirable counterpart because the former behavior is more effective in obtaining social attention. These findings would immediately suggest a course of treatment action, namely, shifting the social attention contingencies such that the desirable class of behavior now receives the greatest proportion of attention.

Unfortunately, little assessment data have accumulated with regard to the maintenance of deviant behavior. Most investigators have monitored only deviant classes of behavior and have been content to prove that adults and peers can establish reinforcement control over the child's behavior. Whereas such findings certainly indicate that these attention dispensers have reinforcement value for the child, they allow only speculation as to how these people supported the child's deviant behavior prior to treatment.

A few investigators have attempted observational assessments of maintenance factors in children's deviant behaviors. The outcomes, although not consistent, do tend to support reinforcement theory. It appears that delinquent peers attend primarily to the deviant actions of other delinquent children (Buehler, Patterson, & Furness, 1966; Duncan, 1969). With reference to teachers, two investigators discovered that teachers provide attention primarily to the deviant behaviors of their problem children (Hall, Lund, & Jackson, 1968; Wahler, 1969b). However, Madsen, Becker, and Thomas (1968) found this relationship for only one of two teachers studied. Findings on parent support of deviant child behavior are much like those concerning teachers. Zeilberger, Sampen, and Sloane (1968) and Wahler (1969b) reported consistently greater proportions of maternal attention following the deviant behaviors of the problem children studied. On the other hand, Wahler, Winkel, Peterson, and Morrison, (1965) found that deviant and desirable child behaviors received about equal amounts of maternal attention.

These few studies considered, it seems likely that deviant child behavior can be maintained by factors more complex than differential amounts of social attention. For example, it could be argued that deviant behavior might obtain less social attention than its desirable counterpart, yet be maintained at greater strength because of some unique scheduling phenomenon or because attention following the desirable behavior is aversive to the child. Whereas these possibilities are intriguing, they have attracted little research attention.

Thus, although available data do point to differential social attention as a factor in the occurrence of deviant child behavior, the clinician should not expect his assessments to reveal such maintenance factors in all cases. This warning is given not only because of the previously reviewed findings, but also because of recent data accumulated by the author. In the author's experience, some deviant behaviors occur in the absence of reliable social contingencies. For example, Wahler, Sperling, Thomas, Teeter, & Luper (1970) discovered that the stuttering behavior of children could *not* be related to parental social attention contingencies. More recently, the author attempted a functional analysis of the strange rituals of a psychotic child. Whereas adult social attention was found to occur contingent upon this behavior, the behavior was attended to less often than were other behavior classes that occurred with lower frequencies. Furthermore, when the adults were trained to ignore the rituals, this operation was found to have no effect on the behavior. Fortunately, it did prove possible to reduce the frequency of this deviant behavior by shaping an incompatible class of the child's desirable behavior. Despite this therapeutic success, however, factors responsible for the maintenance of the rituals remained unknown.

In view of many studies demonstrating the therapeutic power of systematically applied social attention, one conclusion about the above assessment problems seems inevitable: although it may not prove possible (presently) to discover factors responsible for the maintenance of some deviant child behaviors, this situation should not prevent the implementation of treatment programs. In other words, deviant behaviors occurring for unknown reasons might yet be controlled through the proper arrangement of social contingencies in the child's environment. The next section of this paper will describe some of these arrangements.

TREATMENT TACTICS FOR DEVIANT BEHAVIOR

Most social treatment tactics are based on the assumption that community members significant to the deviant child (e.g., parents and teachers) are sources of positive reinforcement for him. Based on this assumption, the clinician normally attempts to rearrange the social attention contingencies set by these community members for the deviant child. Thus, a mother might be instructed to become inattentive whenever her child produces deviant behaviors and to become very attentive following designated desirable behaviors. If the attention dispensed by these community members is indeed reinforcing for the child, such a procedure should have therapeutic effects. Since the child's desirable behavior is now the most effective means of obtaining social reinforcement, this behavior should soon replace his deviant actions.

Research support for these treatment tactics is clear. A large number of investigators have shown that parents (e.g., Hawkins, Peterson, Schweid, & Bijou, 1966), teachers (e.g., Madsen *et al.*, 1968), and peers (e.g., Wahler, 1967) can, by following these simple rules, produce dramatic changes in deviant child behavior. Thus, these treatment tactics seem to fit nicely with some of the previously discussed assessment data. Since parents, teachers, and peers may support deviant child behavior through their differential social attention, they ought to be able to remedy the problem behavior through the same process.

Recently, however, the author has presented data that question the effectiveness of differential attention as a treatment tactic for some child behaviors. Children who are best described as highly oppositional to parental requirements do not seem to improve following parental use of the differential attention tactic (Wahler, 1968). The children in this study were referred for outpatient treatment because of their consistent refusals to comply with parental requests or commands. [These children might also be described as "conduct problems" after Becker (1960).] Unfortunately, parental ignoring of the children's oppositional actions and attending to their cooperative behavior did little to change the frequency of either behavior class. Success was obtained only when the parents applied a punishment contingency (time-out) to the oppositional behavior, as well as continuing to provide approval for cooperative behavior.

Reasons for the ineffectiveness of the differential attention tactic are presently unclear but may be related to parental reinforcement value. In the author's speculation, scheduling parental attention following the children's cooperative behavior had no effect because the parents were of little reinforcement value to the children. That is, perhaps after years of mutually aversive interactions, neither parent nor child found much pleasure in each other's company. Our observations of social interactions between oppositional children and their parents support this speculation. Except for parental attempts to require obediance from the children, or demanding behavior from the children, there were few instances of social interplay between parent and child. It is not uncommon for these parents to provide reports such as this one from a long-suffering mother: "I love my child, but I don't like him."

Thus, because the differential attention tactic proved impractical in controlling the oppositional children, we felt justified in using a time-out contingency. The parents were now instructed to isolate their children (usually in a bedroom) immediately following their oppositional actions. Durations of the time-out periods rarely exceeded five minutes. As previously stated, the use of this contingency produced marked reductions in the children's oppositional behavior. Of greater interest, however, were the more general changes in parent-child interactions. The children approached their parents more frequently and, according to another commonly used test of social reinforcement value (Gewirtz & Baer, 1958), the parents were of greater reinforcement value to the children

(Wahler, 1969a). Apparently, the time-out contingency had indirect as well as direct therapeutic benefits.

Other investigators dealing with highly oppositional children (e.g., Patterson, Cobb, & Ray, 1970) have reported similar therapeutic benefits from the use of time-out. Although this contingency is punitive, it may well be a critical part of behavior modification procedures for such children. Thus, if differential social attention fails to produce therapeutic changes in the child's deviant behavior, the clinician must consider other tactics. Certainly time-out is not the only alternative tactic; other investigators have demonstrated the effectiveness of nonsocial (tokens) means of controlling oppositional children (Phillips, 1968). However, for rapid therapeutic effects and to possibly increase the reinforcement value of the attention dispenser, time-out has much to recommend it.

THE GENERALIZATION OF TREATMENT EFFECTS

Generalization is a phenomenon of central importance in most behavior modification programs. Although all behavior modification workers take measures to deal directly with the problem behaviors of their patients, generalization remains a tacit assumption in considering the goals of treatment. The importance of this assumption depends on the complexity of the child's behavior problem and the complexity of the environments in which the problems occur. For example, if the problem consists of a few simply defined behaviors (e.g., thumb-sucking), occurring in a single stimulus setting (e.g., when watching television), generalization is not an important factor in considering treatment goals. However, the majority of childhood behavior problems are not this simple, and the settings in which they occur are more numerous. Since it is often impractical to arrange contingencies for all of the child's problem behaviors in all environmental settings, the clinician usually depends on generalization to aid the treatment process. This means that significant community members (e.g., parents) would be trained to modify only those problem behaviors for which they can systematically set contingencies. The child's other problems might be expected to improve, both because the child's newly developed desirable behaviors may affect his behavioral repertoire and because of hypothesized general changes in the community member's methods of dispensing attention. It would be wise to examine the empirical support for these assumptions.

Investigations of generalization in child behavior therapy may conveniently be split into two types: (1) those dealing with the generalization of treatment effects within specific environments and (2) those dealing with the generalization of treatment effects across specific environments. Whereas little data have been generated by either type of investigation, most of the studies have been of the first type. These studies will be considered first.

Within-environment generalization has a high likelihood of occurring. In such situations the community members of the environment (e.g., home) have, through behavior modification training, changed their social contingencies for some of the deviant child's behavior. Thus, not only have the community members (e.g., parents) altered their stimulus characteristics, but some of the child's deviant behavior should be altered as well. Generalization possibilities therefore exist along the child behavior dimension and along the stimulus control dimension. On the stimulus control side, the community members may begin to apply their reinforcement techniques to deviant child behaviors other than those they were trained to modify; on the child behavior side, programmed changes in some of his deviant responses might affect similar deviant responses in his behavioral repertoire.

Through either or both of these possibilities, within-environment generalization appears to be a fairly reliable byproduct of behavior modification. Patterson and his associates (Patterson et al., 1970) have obtained clear evidence of this phenomenon in home settings. Following their successful training of parents as behavior modifiers, observational data showed therapeutic changes in the deviant children's target behaviors (those treated directly by the parents) as well as changes in the children's nontarget deviant behaviors. Even more impressive was the finding that the deviant child's siblings also displayed improvements in their problem behaviors. As argued by Patterson, this latter finding would point to changes in parental behavior as the critical factor in producing generalization in home settings. Other generalization evidence involving deviant children has been reported in a school environment (Buell, Baer, Harris, & Stoddard, 1968), in a laboratory environment (Risley, 1968), and in a clinic environment (Wahler & Pollio, 1968).

It seems reasonable to argue that within-environment generalization is largely due to general changes in the community members' methods of dispensing attention to the deviant child. As of yet, however, direct evidence in support of this explanation, as well as any other explanation, is lacking. For example, Wahler et al. (1970) were able to modify the stuttering behavior of children by training their parents to set new social contingencies for other classes of the children's deviant behavior. The stuttering was reduced following this procedure, but an examination of parental social contingencies for the stuttering showed no change before and after implementing the procedure. Thus, while within-environment generalization does occur, factors responsible for the phenomenon remain unclear.

Across-environment generalization seems an unlikely possibility. If child behavior is an important function of its immediate environmental contingencies, one would assume that the behavior is situation specific. A child's behavior at home should be appropriate to the social contingencies set by his parents and siblings; his behavior at school should be governed by teacher and peer contingencies; on the playground, peer social attention might be the important factor controlling his actions.

With these speculations in mind, the benefits of training the child's parents as therapists would be expected at home, but not in those environments where the parents are excluded. Unless community members in the other environments also alter their contingencies for the child, his behavior should remain unchanged in these settings. This somewhat pessimistic viewpoint on generalization has received empirical inquiry.

The author (Wahler, 1969b) studied two children, both of whom presented problems in home and school settings. Assessment observations revealed that the children's parents and teachers were primarily attentive to the deviant actions of the children, thus supporting the hypothesis of parent and teacher maintenance of the deviant behavior. To evaluate across-environment generalization, behavior modification procedures were initiated only in the home setting. Following the successful training of the parents as behavior modifiers, predictable therapeutic changes occurred in the children's home behaviors. Unfortunately, their deviant actions in the school settings remained unchanged, as did teacher social contingencies for the behavior. Only when the teachers were trained to shift their social contingencies to the children's desirable behaviors, did therapeutic benefits become evident at school. Similar failures to obtain across-environment generalization have been reported by Ebner (1967), Alper (1969), and Brodsky (1967).

In view of these data, it is apparent that behavior modification procedures are effective only insofar as community members in the child's various environments practice the procedures. By the time that most children are referred for psychological help they have had ample training to discriminate and to respond appropriately to reinforcement contingencies set by their home, school, and playground environments. Thus, it should not be surprising to discover that changing the contingencies in one of these environments does not alter the child's behavior in other environments. It is possible that newly considered techniques such as "self control" (Goldiamond, 1969) may provide ways to bridge the gap between environments. Presently, however, the clinician should recognize the importance of constructing treatment programs for all environments in which the child's behavior is considered deviant.

FUTURE TRENDS

The generalization issue is probably of utmost importance in future behavior modification research. It may become necessary to face the task of developing comprehensive community programs involving homes, schools, and other major child environments. Clearly, it is not sufficient to deal with only one of these environments with the hope that therapeutic benefits will spread neatly across the child's social world. Unless new procedures can be devised to produce such effects, the concept of "community behavior modification" must be considered seriously.

However, before extending modification procedures to any great extent, it would perhaps be wise to better understand the child's natural interactions with his community. As previously mentioned, the ways in which people in the child's community support his deviant behavior or fail to support his more desirable behavior are not well understood. Only a handful of investigators have even been concerned with this problem. While such understanding does not appear to be a necessary step in constructing treatment programs, it might provide more effective methods of treating and perhaps even preventing childhood behavior disorders. For whatever reasons deviant behavior occurs, it is apparent that some of these behaviors are quite stable over long time periods (e.g., Robins, 1966). If we assume that such behaviors are developed and maintained by interactions with other people, it stands to reason that these natural interactions should be studied carefully. The key to constructing stable therapeutic contingencies for child behavior might lie in knowing how parents, teachers, and peers construct such stable pathological contingencies.

SUMMARY

This paper outlines some principles and tactics of child behavior modification—the assessment and treatment of deviant child behavior as it occurs in natural settings. From this point of view the clinician is seen as a consultant who trains parents, teachers, and peers to function as behavior modifiers. His goals are to understand how the child's social environment supports his deviant behavior and, based partly on this information, how this support might be removed and shifted to the child's more desirable behavior. Despite the theoretical simplicity of behavior modification, attaining these goals is seen as a complex problem.

REFERENCES

Alper, T. A. A comparison of two different treatment approaches for the behavior problems of elementary school children. Unpublished doctoral dissertation, University of Oregon, 1969.

Bandura, A. *Principles of behavior modification.* New York: Holt, 1968.

Barker, R. G. Explorations in ecological psychology. *American Psychologist,* 1965, **20**, 1-14.

Barker, R. G., & Wright, H. F. *Midwest and its children.* New York: Harper, 1955.

Becker, W. C. The relationship of factors in parental ratings of self and each other to the behavior of kindergarten children as rated by mothers, fathers and teachers. *Journal of Consulting Psychology,* 1960, **24**, 507-527.

Bijou, S. W., & Baer, D. M. *Child development. Vol. I. A systematic and empirical theory.* New York: Appleton, 1961.

Bijou, S. W., Peterson, R. F., & Ault, M. H. A method to integrate descriptive and experimental field studies at the level of data and empirical concepts. *Journal of Applied Behavior Analysis,* 1968, **1**, 175-191.

Brodsky, G. The relation between verbal and non-verbal behavior change. *Behavior Research and Therapy.* 1967 **5** 183-192.

Buehler, R. E., Patterson, G. R., & Furness, R. M. The reinforcement of behavior in institutional settings. *Behavior Research and Therapy,* 1966, **4**, 157-167.

Buell, J., Stoddard, P., Harris, F. R., & Baer, D. M. Collateral social development accompanying reinforcement of outdoor play in a preschool child. *Journal of Applied Behavior Analysis,* 1968, **1**, 167-173.

Duncan, D. F. Verbal behavior in a detention home. Unpublished manuscript, Juvenile Hall, Olatha, Kansas, 1969.

Ebner, M. An investigation of the role of the social environment in the generalization and persistence of the effect of a behavior modification program. Unpublished doctoral dissertation, University of Oregon, 1967.

Gewirtz, J. L., & Baer, D. M. Deprivation and satiation of social reinforcers as drive conditions. *Journal of Abnormal and Social Psychology*, 1958, 57, 165-172.

Goldiamond, I. Justified and unjustified alarm over behavioral control. In O. H. Milton and R. G. Wahler (Eds.), *Behavior disorders: Perspectives and trends*. Philadelphia, Pennsylvania: Lippincott, 1969. Pp. 235-240.

Hall, R. V., Jackson, D., & Lund, D. Effects of teacher attention on study behavior. *Journal of Applied Behavior Analysis*, 1968, 1, 1-12.

Hawkins, R. P., Peterson, R. F., Schweid, E., & Bijou, S. W. Behavior therapy in the home: Amelioration of problem parent-child relations with the parent in a therapeutic role. *Journal of Experimental Child Psychology*, 1966, 4, 99-107.

Lovitt, T. C., & Curtis, K. A. Academic response rate as a function of teacher and self-imposed contingencies. *Journal of Applied Behavior Analysis*, 1969, 2, 49-53.

Madsen, C., Becker, W., & Thomas, D. Rules, praise and ignoring: Elements of elementary classroom control. *Journal of Applied Behavior Analysis*, 1968, 1, 139-150.

Patterson, G. R., Cobb, J. A., & Ray, R. S. A social engineering technology for retraining aggressive boys. In H. Adams and L. Unikel (Eds.) *Georgia symposium in experimental clinical psychology*, Vol. II. Oxford: Pergamon, 1970.

Phillips, E. L. Achievement place: Token reinforcement procedures in a home-style rehabilitation setting for "pre-delinquent" boys. *Journal of Applied Behavior Analysis*, 1968, 1, 213-223.

Risley, T. R. The effects and side effects of punishing the autistic behaviors of a deviant child. *Journal of Applied Behavior Analysis*, 1968, 1, 21-34.

Robins, L. N. *Deviant children grown up: A sociological and psychiatric study of sociopathic personality*. Baltimore, Maryland: Williams & Wilkins, 1966.

Wahler, R. G. Child-child interactions in free field settings, some experimental analyses. *Journal of experimental Child Psychology*, 1967, 5, 278-293.

Wahler, R. G. Behavior therapy with oppositional children: Love is not enough. Paper presented at the meeting of the Eastern Psychological Association, Washington, D.C., April, 1968.

Wahler, R. G. Oppositional children: A quest for parental reinforcement control. *Journal of Applied Behavior Analysis*, 1969, 2, 159-170. (a)

Wahler, R. G. Setting generality: Some specific and general effects of child behavior therapy. *Journal of Applied Behavior Analysis*, 1969, 2, 239-246. (b)

Wahler, R. G., & Cormier, W. H. The ecological interview; a first step in outpatient child behavior therapy. *Journal of Behavior Therapy and Experimental Psychiatry*, 1970, 1, 293-303.

Wahler, R. G., & Erickson, M. Child behavior therapy: A community program in Appalachia. *Behavior Research and Therapy*, 1969, 7, 71-78.

Wahler, R. G., Sperling, K. A., Thomas, M. R., Teeter, N. C., & Luper, H. L. The modification of childhood stuttering: Some response-response relationships. *Journal of Experimental Child Psychology*, 1970, 9, 411-428.

Wahler, R. G., Peterson, R. F., Winkel, G. H., & Morrison, D. C. Mothers as behavior therapists for their own children. *Behavior Research and Therapy*, 1965, 3, 113-124.

Wahler, R. G., & Pollio, H. R. Behavior and insight: A case study in child behavior therapy. *Journal of Experimental Research in Personality*, 1968, 4, 105-118.

Zeilberger J., Sampen, S. E., & Sloane, H. N., Jr. Modification of a child's problem behaviors in the home with the mother as therapist. *Journal of Applied Behavior Analysis*, 1968, 1, 47-53.

Discussion: The Role of Parents and Peers in Controlling Children's Behavior

JORGE PERALTA

According to Wahler, observation of the conditions under which a child displays deviant behavior often reveals a variable pattern of setting occasions. The discovery of the stimulus settings is important because it facilitates the solution of two basic problems in designing a program of behavior change. The first is that of limiting the observation to the specific deviant behavior, and the second is the training of those members of the social group who exert control over the child's behavior.

Wahler suggests that interviewing the parents and teachers may be the first step in exploring the stimulus conditions that increase the probability of occurrence of a deviant behavior. It may be of interest to evaluate the effectiveness of interviews with the kind of population frequently seeking psychological consultation in Latin-American countries. Of a sample of 162 who came for help to the Behavior Clinic, an institution that offers psychological services in the city of Xalapa, 27.2% of the mothers and 14.1% of the fathers were illiterate; 3.8% of the sample had attended only one year of elementary school; 19% of the parents had completed elementary school; and .75% had had some degree of professional training. Since these figures are probably fairly typical of Latin-American countries, the low educational level should be taken into account when using the interview as an exploratory technique.

Regarding the identification of stimulus conditions that set the occasion for deviant behavior, Wahler considers this to provide a guideline for the training of those members of the child's natural environment who will function as modifiers of his behavior. He points out that if deviant behaviors are observed to occur under different settings within a specific environment, the psychologist has the option of starting the modification program with the situation that presents the least training problems. It is also important to consider the settings in which the modifier's behavior will be most reinforcing, since the success of a behavior modification program is highly dependent upon the establishment of effective reinforcement contingencies for the parent, teacher, or peers who control the child's behavior.

ASSESSING DEVIANT BEHAVIOR

Wahler states that both the desirable and the undesirable behaviors must be observed when deviant behavior is being evaluated. The frequencies of occurrence in each of these categories are recorded, as well as their social consequences. The author feels that this type of evaluation gives too narrow a view of the problem because it does not provide an account of the (proposed) modifier's behavior and the contingencies that are maintaining it. Observation of the contingencies maintaining the modifier's behavior would give a more complete view of the functional relationship between the child's deviant behavior and all of the contingencies provided by the natural social environment.

To illustrate, let us assume a situation in which the child performs a desirable response which is closely followed by the mother's attention and verbalizations of approval. The behavioral record would indicate good contingency management by the mother. However, the record would not indicate the possibility that another person, perhaps the father, was present during the interaction and was indicating or presenting some other aversive stimulation. It is important to keep in mind such a possibility since it may be the determinant for the failure of the intervention program unless we record it and provide the appropriate contingencies.

The proposed recording technique would provide us with a clearer understanding of the behavior of some parents or teachers who appear unmotivated to use programs to eliminate undesirable behaviors in their children or pupils. If we have records of the contingencies operating upon the modifier, we can manipulate them in order to effect a change in the child's behavior. Recent work by Ayllon, Smith, & Rogers (1972, in press) is an example in point. In this case, the deviant behavior of a child was made aversive to his mother in order to increase the probability that she would apply the contingencies programmed to eliminate the child's problem behavior.

One aspect of the assessment phase, which may be important, is the exploration of reinforcing elements for the child in terms of material reinforcers, social reinforcers, and prepotent responses. According to Tharp and Wetzel (1969), this type of data is utilized when a behavior modification program is implemented in the natural environment. Another aspect not directly mentioned is the assessment of the behavioral repertoire of the deviant child. This is of particular importance when working with subjects who have developmental deficiencies, since the child's deviant behavior may in fact be based upon his behavioral deficits. Establishment of behaviors such as imitation or following instructions may greatly facilitate the implementation of a behavior modification program. Whenever practicable, evaluation of the child's repertoire should be amenable to the use of already available programs so that training can proceed from the point indicated by the assessment data.

Wahler points out that few data are available concerning the maintenance of deviant behavior, especially for those cases in which the behavior seems to be maintained by factors other than differential amounts of social attention. Tharp and Wetzel (1969) have pointed out that stealing behavior can be maintained by its direct lateral contingencies. Patterson (1971, personal communication) has indicated that aggressive behavior may be directly reinforced by the behavior of the person being attacked, without the intervention of other agents in the social environment. It is the author's contention that further research is needed concerning other types of reinforcers which may be maintaining deviant behavior.

TREATMENT TECHNIQUES FOR DEVIANT BEHAVIOR

Wahler considers the basic training technique for modifying children's deviant behavior to be the manipulation of attention and social reinforcement—making them contingent upon desirable behavior and withholding them when undesirable behavior is observed. We would like to suggest the relevance of the triadic model proposed by Tharp and Wetzel (1969) and involving the advisor, the mediator, and the target. Under the direction of the advisor, the mediator, who may be any member(s) of the child's natural environment, controls the reinforcing events for the child. It is important to realize that the success of the treatment program depends not only upon the specific arrangement of contingencies for the child but also upon the contingencies provided for the mediator. In this regard, Tharp and Wetzel (1969) state that reinforcement for the mediator may arise from several environmental sources such as the following: the advisor, the behavior changes produced in the problem child, and those elements integrating the mediator's social environment. At present, there is very little data about the strength of each of these reinforcers in maintaining the mediator's behavior. Thus, the triadic model should be considered as a conceptual one, requiring more data to support its validity.

We would like to emphasize that a good behavior modification program in the natural environment is one that specifies a careful arrangement of the contingencies provided for both the mediator and the target child. An example of this type of intervention program is the pioneer work of Patterson (1965a), in which the peers of a hyperactive child functioned as mediators to increase the time he spent in his seat. The mediators were reinforced every time the problem child engaged in the target behavior and, at the same time, they reinforced the problem child with applause and social approval. If we are able to establish the target as a reinforcing event for the peer, parent, teacher, etc., there is a high probability that this behavior will be maintained.

Another of the suggested reinforcers for maintaining the mediator's behavior is the feedback provided by the behavior changes of the deviant child. Panyan, Boozer, and Morris (1970) have shown that this kind of contingency was effective in maintaining the mediator's behavior in a program with institutionalized children. Tharp and Wetzel (1969) and Patterson and Cobb (1970) have pointed out that another potential source of reinforcement for the mediator's behavior is praise from other members of the community (e.g., neighbors, relatives, or friends). It seems to the author that future technological development will require the direct measurement and manipulation of these sources of reinforcement as they operate upon the mediator's behavior.

Another important finding pointed out by Wahler is that differential attention is not always an effective means of eliminating undesirable behavior. A direct measure of attention as a reinforcing event is reported in only a few cases, such as by Patterson (1965b), who pointed out that adult attention was not a strong enough reinforcing event to maintain the child's behavior and that it was necessary to use candies as an initial contingency in order to establish control over the child's behavior. According to the theory of human development (Bijou & Baer, 1961), attention does function as a reinforcing event; however, one must be aware of the possibility of a past history of aversive social interactions between the mediator and the deviant child. A history of aversive interactions would greatly reduce the reinforcing function of the mediator's attention; thus, it is imperative to evaluate the reinforcing value of attention before using it in a behavior-change program.

On the other hand, it is also possible to explore the effectiveness of other types of reinforcing events available within the child's natural environment: for example, prepotent activities (Homme, Homme, & De Baca, 1958; Homme & Tosti, 1965), the direct manipulation of setting events that increase the value of a reinforcing event (Bijou & Baer, 1961), and a change in activities (Risley, Reynolds, & Hart, 1970). What we would like to emphasize is the necessity of extending the range of manipulable reinforcing events within the technology of behavior change, in order to have available greater resources when planning an intervention program.

Wahler states in chapter 2, this volume, that punishment seems to increase the value of social reinforcement. This effect was observed by McReynolds (1969), who found that after a period of time in the program the effect of social reinforcement decreased, as evidenced by a deterioration in the subject's performance. When the aversive time-out contingency was applied to the behavior, a new increase in the value of the social reinforcement was observed. According to McReynolds, this effect is found only when both the social and the aversive contingencies are applied by the same person. In his work with several children, Ribes-Inesta, (1971, personal communication) has noted the effectiveness of aversive stimulation. One negativistic child showed an increase in social responses to the experimenter after the introduction of punishment for his aggressive responses. Another negativistic child, identified as a case of selective mutism, received an electric shock every time he did not emit the required verbal response. This procedure resulted in a significant increase in the child's verbal behavior, which was then maintained by social reinforcement. Although not all of this work can be called systematic, the overall picture indicates the importance of further investigation of the effects of aversive stimulation on the value of social reinforcement.

GENERALIZATION OF THE EFFECTS OF TREATMENT

One of the most important goals is the generalization of the obtained behavior changes to other situations. Here, Wahler makes a distinction between two types of generalization of treatment effects: first, generalization of effects within a specific environment and, second, the generalization of effects across different environments. He also points out that generalization of treatment effects may be related to two sources: the child's recently acquired desirable behaviors, which may affect his other behaviors, and the changed modes by which members of the community respond to the child's behaviors. After the members of the community have been trained to deal with certain problem behaviors, they often begin applying these social contingencies to other deviant behaviors as well. Wahler presents empirical data to support the phenomenon of generalization within a specific environment as a reliable outcome of behaivor modification programs. However, the specific factors responsible for this generalization are still unclear. It is the author's belief that the explanation will be obtained by carefully recording the interactions between the child and the mediator.

Wahler maintains that the probability of generalization across different environments is low, since the conditions for behavioral change depend upon the specific environmental contingencies carried out by the members of the community. The situational specificity of behavioral change must be taken into account in the implementation of intervention programs, especially with children evidencing deviant behaviors in several different environments. And, of course, there remains the possibility of developing new techniques that will permit greater generalization of the treatment effects.

PROGRAMS FOR PREVENTING DEVIANT BEHAVIORS

Finally, Wahler suggests the usefulness of developing preventive techniques for deviant behaviors. The first steps in this direction have already been taken. Ulrich, Wolf, and Cole (1970), Risley, Reynolds, and Hart (1970), and Peralta and Leon (1970) have developed programs aimed toward the establishment of behavior repertoires required by society in general and by the educational system in particular.

With these goals in mind, the author has been working with a group of 12 children in a nursery school setting. The evaluation of precurrent repertoires (e.g., imitative behavior, following instructions, auditory and visual discriminations) is based on available programs that were originally designed for use with another population (Ribes-Inesta & De Souza e Silva, 1971). One goal that should be emphasized is the establishment of verbal repertoires appropriate to the requirements of the school system. Our preliminary data indicate that these children have a limited verbal repertoire, i.e., they make frequent use of slang terms that are appropriate only in certain nonschool environments.

The children in the research program are exposed to situations similar to those of a preschool setting. The classroom has several partitioned areas, each containing manipulable objects and academic materials that facilitate verbal behavior. We have kept the environment as "natural" as possible by providing sources that are compatible with the children's environment. On the other hand, children are also exposed to group situations resembling those of a regular classroom wherein several school-type behaviors are recorded, as for example, being out of the seat, attending behavior, talking in appropriate situations, etc. After this recording phase, contingencies will be established to increase the types of behaviors that are required in the regular school situation.

We have just started this program, and it is possible that several aspects will require changing. In Latin-American countries, where economical resources are scarce, the preventive approach and manipulation of the elements within the natural environment appear to be wise alternatives to remedying problem behaviors. The prevention of behavioral disorders on a greater scale must include the systematic education and training of all who play a role, small or great, in the development and maintenance of human behavior. To achieve this end, the educational and economic systems must be radically overhauled, since these systems exert control over many reinforcers in the society. It is only when such societal changes have occurred, and an exact and well-developed technology is available, that the goal of a much improved society will be realized.

REFERENCES

Ayllon, T., Smith, D., & Rogers, M. Behavioral management of school phobia. *Journal of Behaviour Research & Therapy*, 1972, in press.

Bijou, S. W., & Baer, D. M. *Child development: A systematic and empirical theory.* Vol. 1. New York: Appleton, 1961.

Bijou, S. W., & Baer, D. M. *Child development: Universal stage of infancy.* Vol. 2. New York: Appleton, 1965.

Homme, L. E., Homme, A., & De Baca, P. What behavioral engineering is. *Psychological Record*, 1968, 18, 425-434.

Homme, L. E., & Tosti, D. T. Contingency management and motivation. *National Society for Programmed Instruction Journal*, 1965, 4, (7).

McReynolds, L. V. Application of time-out from positive reinforcement. *Journal of Applied Behavior Analysis*, 1969, 2, 199-205.

Panyan, M., Boozer, H., & Morris, N. Feedback to attendants as a reinforcer for applying operant techniques. *Journal of Applied Behavior Analysis*, 1970, 3, 1-4.

Patterson, G. R. Responsiveness to social stimuli. In L. Krasner and L. Ullman (Eds.), *Research in behavior modification.* New York: Holt, 1965.   (a)

Patterson, G. R. The modification of hyperactive behaviors. In L. Ullman and L. Krasner (Eds.), *Case studies in behavior modification.* New York: Holt, 1965.   (b)

Patterson, G. R., & Cobb, J. A. A dyadic analysis of aggressive behaviors. In J. Hill (Ed.), *Proceedings of the Fifth Minnesota Symposium on Child Psychology.* Minneapolis, Minn.: Univ. of Minnesota, 1970. Pp. 72-129.

Peralta, J., & Leon, A. L. El desarrollo de un programa de prevencion de desordenes conductuales en pre-escolares. Clinica de Conducta, Univ. of Veracruz, 1970.

Ribes-Inesta, E., & De Souza e Silva, S. An extensive behavioral rehabilitation program for retarded children. Unpublished manuscript, Univ. of Veracruz, 1971.

Risley, T. R., Reynolds, N., & Hart, B. Behavior modification with disadvantaged pre-school children. In R. Bradfield (Ed.), *Behavior modification: A most human endeavor.* San Rafael, California: Dimensions Publ. Co., 1970.

Tharp, W., & Wetzel, R. J. *Behavior modification in natural environment.* New York: Academic Press, 1969.

Ulrich, R., Wolf, M., & Cole, R. Early education: A preventive mental health program. *Michigan Mental Health Bulletin*, 1970, 4, (1).

The Technology of Teaching Young Handicapped Children[1]

SIDNEY W. BIJOU

For many years, about 75 in fact, enormous amounts of time, energy, and money have been expended on problems associated with the early education of the retarded and emotionally disturbed child. Unfortunately, the outcome of these efforts has been less than gratifying. Recent surveys have shown that special classes for the handicapped child have been no more effective than the regular elementary classes. Johnson (1962), discussing the problem, stated pointedly that special classes have failed because special teachers have devoted themselves to matters other than those that constitute their main mission—teaching academic skills.

> During the past three decades the general orientation of teacher preparation programs for the mentally handicapped has been (a) an emphasis upon disability rather than ability and (b) the necessity for establishing a "good" mental hygiene situation for the children where they can develop into emotionally healthy individuals. Thus, the pressures for learning and achievement have been largely removed so that the child has no need to progress [Johnson, 1962, p. 68].

[1]The research described here is supported by the U.S. Office of Education, Division of Research, Bureau of Education for the Handicapped, Project No. 5-0961, Grant No. OEG32-23-6002.

27

   Casual observation and discussions with special teachers bear out the con-
tention that there is indeed too little attention given to teaching tool subjects,
the justification for this practice seeming to be based on a hiatus between
teaching and learning and static concepts of intelligence and retardation.

   Recently, the art of teaching and the science of learning have been merged
into a technology of teaching (Skinner, 1968), and intelligence and retardation
have been analyzed as behavioral deficits resulting from biological, physical, and
social restrictions in opportunities for development (Bijou, 1966a). One series of
studies following this orientation has concentrated on the development of
educational procedures for the institutionalized retarded child (Bijou, 1965;
Bijou, 1966b; Bijou, Birnbrauer, Kidder, & Tague, 1966; Birnbrauer, Kidder, &
Tague, 1964; Birnbrauer, Wolf, Kidder, & Tague, 1965; and Birnbrauer & Lawler,
1964). Another sequence of investigations has focused on treatment techniques
of the young, emotionally disturbed child (Hawkins, Peterson, Schweid, & Bijou
1966; Risley & Wolf, 1967; Sloane, Johnston, & Bijou 1967; Sloane &
MacAulay, 1968; and Wolf, Risley, & Mees, 1964).

   Findings from these studies have provided the underpinnings for the research
at the University of Illinois, the main objective of which is to fabricate a
technology for teaching young school children with serious behavior problems.
Our research project has two aspects: one centers on developing, in successive
stages, an integrated set of classroom materials, a flexible curriculum format, and
an explicit set of teaching procedures; the other, on investigating problems that
evolve from the technology. We shall describe these operations, summarized
from what we have learned, and point out some specific implications for
teaching the handicapped child.

TOWARD A TECHNOLOGY OF SPECIAL TEACHING

   The process of fabricating a behavioral technology of special teaching has
three characteristics. First, all teaching materials and teaching procedures are
developed in a class of handicapped children and involve the teacher and her
assistant. Second, changes in materials and teaching techniques are based on a
conception of teaching as the arrangement of conditions and contingencies of re-
inforcement that expedite learning (Skinner, 1968). Third, the effectiveness of
each change in evaluated by data obtained from monitoring the performance
of children studied individually.

The Physical Setting

   Two classrooms were architecturally designed to provide the basic needs of a
special classroom and to facilitate observation of the children and the collection
of data. Figure 1 shows both classrooms flanked by an observation room with a
large, one-way viewing screen, recording equipment, and listening devices. Op-
posite the wall with the one-way screen are three small rooms: a toilet room, a
water-play room, and a tutoring room. Each of these interior rooms has a large
window that faces the classroom, enabling the teacher in the main part of the

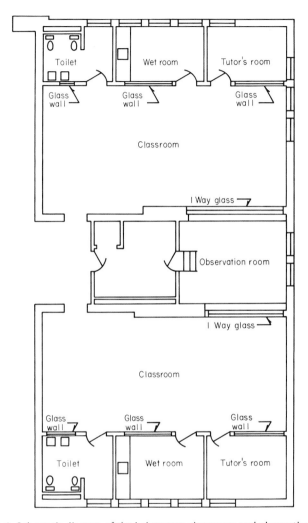

Fig. 1. Schematic diagram of the Laboratory classrooms and observation room.

classroom to observe what is taking place in those adjacent rooms. Desks, chairs, and partitions are portable for maximum flexibility in arranging individual and group teaching situations. Data are collected on individual children in the classroom for carrying out field descriptive studies (e.g., Bijou, Peterson, & Ault, 1968) or field experimental studies (e.g., Peterson, Cox, & Bijou, 1971), or in one of the laboratory rooms on the floor below the classrooms for individual laboratory studies (e.g., Bijou, 1968). The laboratory rooms are shown schematically in Fig. 2. Each room is equipped with a one-way screen and electronic devices for listening and recording.

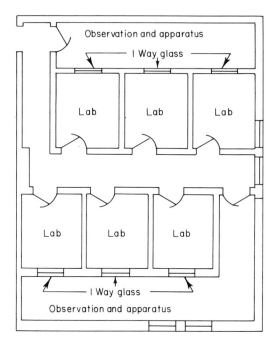

Fig. 2. Schematic diagram of the individual study rooms.

The Children

The children are of kindergarten and primary school age—from five to eight—who have been referred to the Laboratory classes because of serious social and academic problems. Although their handicaps are not so extreme as to require institutional care, they are serious enough to warrant referral of the child to a community treatment agency. The school authorities have described these children as mentally retarded or emotionally disturbed, or as having a learning disability or a serious behavior problem such as being too aggressive or too withdrawn. Here are some examples of the kinds of children admitted.

A six-year-old-boy. He is unresponsive to most of the teacher's requests and spends much time wandering around the room mumbling to himself. He avoids contact with others, frequently cowers in the presence of strangers, and rarely interacts with other children. He does, however, play with certain toys. He recognizes most letters and forms some words with them even though he had never attended school before. His limited speech is primarily echolalic.

A six-year-old girl. She says "No" to almost everything that is asked of her and teases the teacher by doing what she has been forbidden to do when she is sure the teacher is watching her. She does not interact with other children but does play with some toys. She has echolalic speech.

A six-year-old boy. He talks out of turn, runs around the room, kicks, hits, pushes, and interferes verbally and physically with the activities of other children. This obtrusive behavior has resulted in his having been transferred from one public school to another soon after the beginning of the school year and his expulsion from the second school after one week of attendance, whereupon he was referred to the Laboratory school. His academic skills are below beginning kindergarten achievement.

An eight-year-old girl. She is not a behavior problem, but her academic achievement is at beginning first-grade level. Writing is her most advanced skill. In the regular public school she was in the third grade but obviously could not do the work. Her social behavior, too, is below that expected of an eight-year-old.

Functionally speaking, all of the children referred to the Laboratory school are retarded (Bijou, 1966a), i.e., they lack the behavior repertories, academic and social, that schools require of children in kindergarten and the primary grades. But merely to say that they are mentally retarded, or to label them with any other diagnostic term, is of no use to the teacher since these tags do not provide the teacher with the kinds of information she needs to prepare effective instructional programs. Only a detailed inventory of each child's academic and social skills and the sorts of events that motivate academic achievement does that.

The Curriculum

In a technology of teaching, the teacher must have pages of academic materials, workbooks, textbooks, etc., designed for individual instruction on the basis of the performance of a large number of children studied individually. The materials for the various tool subjects, together with their teacher's manual, pre- and posttests, and recording procedures, constitute the formal programs of the curriculum.

The following formal programs are in use and are being further refined and extended.

1. *Writing.* Training proceeds along four progressions, simultaneously:
    (a) from writing on wide-lined and wide-spaced paper to writing on finer-lined, standard primary paper;
    (b) from copying from a model to writing from dictation;
    (c) from writing letters to writing words, phrases, and sentences;
    (d) from printing to writing in script.

If necessary, the program may be preceded by a subprogram on how to hold and how to use a pencil.

2. *Reading.* This program is modeled on the sight vocabulary program of the Rainier School Program (Bijou *et al.,* 1966). Four procedures are involved in learning each new word:
    (a) LC, listening comprehension—to determine whether the child has the word in his listening (receptive) vocabulary;

(b) RD, reading discrimination—to teach the child to discriminate between the new word and other similar words in written form;

(c) RB, readback—to teach the child to read the word aloud when it is presented in written or textual form;

(d) RC, reading comprehension—to teach the child the meaning of new words. A brief discriminated program precedes the reading program to ensure that the child can make the necessary auditory and visual discriminations. Also included in the reading program is a subprogram on simple phonetics to develop word-attack skills (techniques to prompt himself when he does not know how to read the word on sight).

3. *Arithmetic.* This program is also based on the Rainier School Program (Bijou *et al.,* 1966). It begins with the child's saying the names of the numbers and proceeds to counting (chaining) to 20, dot counting, simple addition using his fingers as aids, subtraction, and multiplication. The program also extends into time-telling. The Min-Max teaching machine is used to present some of the units of this program.

4. *Spelling.* Children learn to spell words they have had in the reading program by the following procedures:

(a) copying the words from a typewritten model;

(b) testing themselves with Language Master cards with the correct spelling of the word on the back;

(c) testing themselves with Language Master cards with auditory feedback.

5. *Language.* This program teaches the children the use of common adjectives, prepositions, and verbs; subject-verb agreement; gross time relationships (seasons, months, weeks, etc.); and useful personal information (name, address, phone number). Both group interaction and individual desk work are utilized; children master specific concepts individually at their own rate and learn to utilize the concepts within the larger group.

There are, in addition, several short, specialized programs which aim to prepare a child for the formal reading and arithmetic programs or to supplement the knowledge or skills covered in the programs. For example, there is the plurals program, which systematically prompts the child to add the *s* sound when reading plural nouns.

The classes meet from 8:15 A.M. to 12:30 P.M. daily. As the children arrive, they are greeted by the teacher who serves them breakfast and encourages them to talk about their experiences during the previous afternoon and evening or before coming to school that morning. Relaxed conversations of this sort not only increase communication skills and strengthen social relationships but prime the kinds of social and emotional behaviors that help a child to have a happy and productive school day.

The daily schedule, which is designed to be flexible, is as follows:

8:15- 8:45	Greeting and breakfast time
8:45- 9:10	Study period 1
9:10- 9:35	Study period 2
9:35-10:00	Study period 3
10:00-10:30	Language period
10:30	Store time
10:30-11:00	Recess
11:00-11:30	Study period 4
11:30-12:00	Story, art, and freeplay
12:00	Store time
12:00-12:30	Study period 5

Each child's assignment for each study period, prepared by the teacher and her assistant the afternoon before, is contained in a color-coded folder in his desk. With prompts from the teacher, the child refers to the master chart on the bulletin board for instructions on which folder to use for each period. Not all the children will necessarily be working on the same subject at the same time, and those who are will probably be working at different levels of materials within that subject. Nor will each child get the same amount or kind of help with an assignment. The teacher will help some and the assistant others; and some of the children will work alone, depending on the achievement level and the study skills they have acquired. A typical daily program would be something like this:

Study period 1. *Writing*—copying words from typed cards, working in a small group under the teacher's supervision.

Study period 2. *Arithmetic*—doing simple addition facts, also in a small teacher-supervised group.

Study period 3. *Reading*—learning new words and reading for comprehension, working alone with a tutor.
Language period—working on words and sentences in communication skills with whole class participating.

Study period 4. *Writing*—writing numbers and letters from dictation and reading independently, then writing in a workbook.

Teacher Practices

The key to a technology of special teaching is the behavior of the teacher. Well-programmed units and a well-organized classroom are of little value *unless the teacher manages the conditions at her disposal in ways that expedite learning in each of her pupils*. So we shall dwell on the instructional repertories of a special teacher in a classroom designed to apply behavioral principles.

Techniques of Assessing the Child

In most school systems the school psychologist assesses the abilities and achievements of the child. Using psychometric tests and a modified form of psychoanalytic theory, he attempts to predict the child's performance in class, categorize the cause (etiology) of his problem, and analyze his personality in "dynamic" terms. Little of the information in the psychologist's report is helpful to the teacher in planning an instructional program for the child because, generally, it does not refer to the *specific things* the child can do. Even if the school psychologist were trained to provide the kind of information that is relevant to individual program planning, it would still be preferable for the teacher to evaluate her own pupils. The assessment process gives the teacher first-hand acquaintance with what the child can do, his style of performing, and his responsiveness to social contingencies. This kind of direct knowledge is far more helpful to her than a verbal account by someone whose responsibility to the child is already finished.

In the Laboratory school, the teacher's assessment is based on (1) observational data taken during the child's last day or two in the public school classroom from which he is being removed, and on his behavior during the first week to ten days in the Laboratory classroom; (2) results from the Caldwell Preschool Inventory (Caldwell, 1967); (3) tests from the reading, writing, arithmetic, spelling, and language programs used in the laboratory class; and (4) information from medical and school reports and from interviews with mother, teacher, and school psychologist. From all these sources, the teacher draws conclusions about (a) the child's specific skills and knowledge relative to school work and social behavior, (b) the kinds of social relationships, objects, and activities that are likely to function as reinforcers, and (c) the support she may expect from the parents or guardians. On the basis of this diagnostic summary, she prepares an instructional program for the child.

In addition to making this assessment, the teacher administers at the beginning and end of the school year the Peabody Picture Vocabulary Test (Dunn, 1959) and the Wide Range Achievement Test (Jastak, Bijou, & Jastak, 1965). Findings from these scales, which express the child's performance relative to other children of the same age, provide information that is of interest to teachers and principals and some parents.

Techniques of Program Planning and Modification

To individualize instruction, the teacher must be able not only to plan each child's program but to modify the sequences when a child encounters difficulties with it. Many of the details of program planning and modification can be performed by the teacher's assistant. But whether the teacher works alone or has an assistant, she must know the principles of programmed instruction so that she can modify the program either to avoid assignments that are too difficult and hence lead to a high error rate or assignments that are too easy and result in the kind of aversiveness that comes with sheer repetition of well-learned tasks. In other words, she must know programming principles so that she can adjust the materials to a level slightly above the child's repertorv. A well-trained teacher does not have to consult a programming expert each time one of her children falters.

In the Child Behavior Laboratory, the teacher routinely spends part of her afternoons reviewing the academic progress of each child and preparing assignment folders for the next day. If she finds that a child is not making reasonable progress in a subject, she prepares a remedial sequence, one designed to provide him with skills or knowledge he seems to lack. Remedial sets are discontinued as soon as the child is able to make progress on the regular program at about the 90% level of proficiency.

Techniques of Managing Reinforcement Contingencies

Under the category of managing reinforcement contingencies, we include the procedures for evaluating (a) the effectiveness of reinforcers, (b) the appropriateness of a schedule of reinforcement in light of the target behavior, and (c) the appropriateness of applying contingencies for the task to be learned.

Evaluating the effectiveness of reinforcers for a child is not simple. It requires far more than an impression of what a child likes or what one thinks he should like. It requires extended observation of sequences of the child's interactions with activities to determine which contingencies are functional in keeping the child working on a task. It also requires continuous monitoring of his school work, because the kinds of conditioned reinforcers used in the classroom often change in effectiveness with changes in setting factors and with advances in learning. The teacher cannot assume that once she has identified a class of reinforcers that are functional for a child she has completed the task of "understanding the motivation" of that child. She must be vigilant in seeking new reinforcers that are at least equal to or even more effective than those she is using, if for no other reason than to avoid decreases in proficiency because of satiation with those stimuli.

Evaluating schedules of reinforcement in light of the target or desired terminal behavior calls for a knowledge of the kinds of behavior that are generated when the intermittencies of reinforcing contacts are changed. Schedules are manipulated in order to increase the effectiveness of study behavior. For example, a continuous schedule of reinforcement may be changed to an increasing ratio schedule in an effort to build longer and longer chains of having a child remain seated, paying attention to instructions, carrying out instructions, moving from task to task without dawdling, etc. Or a continuous schedule of reinforcement may be changed to an increasing ratio schedule to encourage working independently and productively, e.g., gradually shifting from reinforcing every correct response on a page to reinforcing every full page of correct responses.

Percentage schedules of reinforcement are also altered to revive old conditioned reinforcers or to develop new ones. By percentage reinforcement schedule, we mean the proportion of time in which the contrived reinforcer (mark, token) is given together with a social reinforcer. At the beginning of the child's enrollment in the classroom, the contrived and social reinforcers are paired 100% of the time, and gradually the percentage is decreased until the social contingency is, by itself, functional. The procedure of weaning the child from contrived contingencies by a percentage reinforcement schedule was evaluated last year at the Laboratory by observing the behavior of the children in one of the classes during the final weeks of school. Recorded for each child were the frequencies of attentive and disruptive behaviors defined as follows: Attentive behavior—eye contact with the teacher or the activity, with the child in his seat. Disruptive behavior—out of seat, away from activity, talking out of turn—judged in relation to the class activity in progress.

Four of the eight children were observed over a period of sixteen days: twelve days with mark-giving in effect and four days without marks being given. Data showed that, during the time marks were in effect, the average percentage of attending behavior was 84.0 and the average percentage of disruptive behavior was 10.3. When the tokens were withdrawn, the average percentage of attending behavior was 80.3 and the average percentage of disruptive behavior was 12.0. Since the elimination of marks did not alter the children's behavior to a significant degree, the mark system was abandoned at that time.

We have discussed, then, the procedures for evaluating the effectiveness of reinforcers and the appropriateness of a schedule of reinforcement for terminal behaviors. We turn now to the third aspect of managing the contingencies of reinforcement that pertains to delivering reinforcers in ways that are appropriate to the behavior to be learned. We are referring here to the differential techniques used (1) to modify the form of a response, such as in writing letters of the alphabet, and (2) to develop new knowledge, such as in reading words. Both types of learning require the child to give a constructed response (writing and saying). However, writing skills are best acquired when contingencies follow *shaping* procedures, whereas learning to read words is most rapidly strengthened when contingencies follow *stimulus control* procedures. To improve a child's writing, the teacher should deliver contingencies for correct and incorrect responses in ways that strengthen the entire form of the response; to enhance his ability to read words, she should manage consequences to increase the probability that the child will give the accepted verbal response when the word is presented visually. We hasten to add that writing and other manual skills, as well, also require stimulus control (e.g., paying attention to the details of the model to be copied), and reading also involves shaping procedures (e.g., learning to articulate words), but the training described here stresses the development of the characteristic aspect of these two types of responses.

Techniques of Modifying Social Behavior and Precurrent Academic Behavior

These are programs that the teacher "carries around in her head." They are aimed at helping the child acquire a repertory serviceable in the school culture, e.g., teaching him to hang up his coat on entering the classroom or encouraging him to try finger painting. These informal programs consist of the skillful use of prompts, cues, and priming techniques to produce the desired behavior, of fading procedures to transfer stimulus control from the training situation to the appropriate set of circumstances, and of schedule changes to maintain the behavior acquired.

A new teacher in the Laboratory classroom is taught these techniques in a kind of clinical case procedure, that is, as they pertain to the behavior and circumstances of an individual child in the class of an experienced behavioral teacher. She is given opportunities to observe the experienced teacher and to discuss with her the objectives for each child and the techniques she uses to achieve them. When the neophyte tries out these practices in her own class, she discusses her successes and failures with members of the staff, usually in an informal conference held at the end of the school day.

Techniques of Monitoring the Daily Activity of Each Child

Recording techniques that provide a monitored account of a child's behavior are an integral part of a behaviorally engineered classroom. The use of monitoring measures follows from a definition of teaching as the arrangement of conditions and reinforcement contingencies to expedite learning and from the fact that the technology of teaching is in the early stages of developing its procedures. Hence, there is a strong and pervasive tendency to use systems that immediately yield information on the effectiveness of any innovation.

In the Laboratory classroom, the teacher and her assistant collect data on each child's progress in the formal academic programs. For example, in the reading and arithmetic programs, data are recorded on errors, the kind or kinds of contingencies applied, and their schedules of contacts. Error rates (percentages) and reinforcement contacts are summarized on data sheets and, from time to time, graphs are prepared to improve the teacher's perspective of the child's performance in these subjects.

Data are also taken on the child's progress on the programs for remediating problem behavior. These records are generally counts of instances or frequencies of occurrence, grouped in prearranged categories.

Techniques of Training the Teacher's Assistant

Even with well-programmed materials, serviceable teaching aids, and a good grasp of the principles of contingency management, the special teacher needs an assistant, a helping hand in individualizing teaching, i.e., in evaluating and preparing each child's assignments and in making the conditions for learning more attractive. She needs an assistant who likes children, who is highly reinforced when a child makes progress, and who is eager to learn new teaching techniques. To be maximally helpful, the assistant should be trained by the teacher with whom she will be working.

In a Laboratory class, the trained assistant is ultimately able to assemble the daily assignments in each subject for each child, to prepare remedial sets, to keep monitored data, to tutor a child, and to supervise individual learning in small group situations. Training, as with a new teacher, starts with the assistant's observing the classroom teacher in action. She is given opportunities first to assist the teacher in tutoring a child, then to tutor under the teacher's supervision, and finally to tutor without supervision. When the teacher is satisfied that her assistant has learned how to establish a pleasant relationship (rapport) with a child, how to use primes, prompts, and contingencies effectively, and how to collect data on the child's progress, the formal apprenticeship in tutoring is terminated.

In addition to the six teaching techniques described, it is desirable, perhaps essential is a more appropriate word, that the teacher have one other qualification: an *optimistic attitude about the learning potential of each of her pupils.* No one would deny that an optimistic attitude in a teacher is preferable to a pessimistic attitude. But in a behavior analysis approach to teaching, this requirement evolves naturally from one of the basic assumptions of the theory, namely, that the behavior one observes in a child is determined by the history of the child and the circumstances at the time he is being observed. Hence, when a child is making reasonable progress in an academic or social program, the materials and the reinforcing contingencies employed are assumed to be adequate for him. On the other hand, when he falters, the materials, the reinforcers, or both are assumed to be inadequate for him. When a child fails to make progress, the course of action is clear: analyze the source of the problem, present a modified set of conditions, monitor the child's performance under the new conditions, and revise the conditions again if necessary until the child shows progress. (Escape hatches attributing lack of progress to mental retardation, learning disability, or some other trait are closed.) The cherished optimistic attitude, therefore, carries with it a willingness to view each problem behavior as a personal challenge in modifying the educational environment so that the undesirable behavior will give way to desirable behavior. Under these circumstances, even the slightest improvement in the child's behavior will be highly reinforcing to the teacher and, as a consequence, she will be more likely to try harder when faced with the next challenge, and will be more convinced than ever that teaching can be a most gratifying and absorbing profession.

FORMAL RESEARCH

The formal investigations undertaken at the Laboratory fall into two groups: those that aim to improve research methodology and those that explore teacher-child and parent-child functional relationships.

Studies on Research Methodology

Three studies on research methodology have concentrated on procedures appropriate for the analysis of behavior in natural settings, such as the classroom, home, or clinic. The first illustrates a method for *describing* the behavior of a child as it occurs naturally and without any experimental manipulation (Bijou *et al.,* 1968). This approach, which is offered as an alternative to describing behavior in the form of verbal statements (e.g., Barker & Wright, 1955) or rating scales (e.g., Baldwin, Kalhorn, & Breeze, 1949), involves (1) specifying the situation in which a study takes place, (2) defining the critical behavioral and environmental events in observable categories, (3) recording the frequencies with which these events occur, (4) estimating observer reliability, and (5) presenting the data in graphic form. These steps are illustrated in a descriptive study of a four-year-old boy attending a university nursery school. The account details the child's sustained activity (on-task behavior) and social interactions during the school activities over a period of 28 days. One of the advantages of the frequency category is that it provides data that can be used, without alteration, for an experimental study in the same situation. That is to say, a descriptive study of this type yields an account of behavior that may in turn serve as a multiple baseline for ferreting out which events are functionally related.

The second paper on research methodology delineates a procedure for experimenting with stimulus and response relationships in natural settings (Bijou, Peterson, Harris, Allen, & Johnston, 1969). It outlines the procedure for defining response and stimulus variables, illustrates workable response and stimulus categories, and suggests ways of establishing baselines, manipulating independent variables, and representing findings.

The third paper describes a method, consistent with the two described above, that may be used to plan and guide educational, therapeutic, and rehabilitation programs (Bijou & Peterson, 1971). Steps are outlined that show how observational techniques may serve to assess the entering repertoires of a child (diagnosis), how to plan the details of his treatment regime, how to monitor his progress, and how to assess the outcome of treatment.

Studies on Teacher-Child and Parent-Child Functional Relationships

Some of the investigations of functional relationships have dealt with teacher-child relationships as they pertain to academic learning in group situations (Peterson, Cox, & Bijou, 1971). The contention is that children can work productively in a classroom group if the foundations for the required behavior are first laid in a one-to-one tutorial situation. Two experiments were performed. The first showed that the high rates of learning developed in a tutorial situation were maintained in a group of two children. The second study demonstrated that the high rates of learning developed in single tutorials were maintained in a group of six children.

Another study on teacher-child relationships was concerned with the multiple effects of reinforcing verbal behavior (Sajwaj, Twardosz, Kantor, & Burke, 1970). The effects of reinforcing the verbal behavior of a seven-year-old retarded boy in a freeplay period were observed both in that period and in the following one—the group-learning period (circle time). During the freeplay period, when the teacher attended to his verbal overtures, the boy's verbal behavior toward her increased, his play with toys was more "girlish" in character, and appropriate peer behavior decreased. During the circle-time group activity that followed (when no special attention was paid him), his appropriate behavior increased, and, conversely, his disruptive behavior decreased. These data suggest that reinforcement of this child's social behavior toward his teacher not only increased the rate of this particular behavior but in the same situation also altered the child's toy-play and peer-play behaviors. That same manipulation, furthermore, resulted in altering the child's behavior in the next class activity. Hence, reinforcement of social behavior in the preceding period was correlated with a higher rate of appropriate group behavior in the succeeding period.

Other studies exploring functional relationships have dealt with problems of parent-child relations in the home. One such investigation centered on the problem behavior of a preschool boy during lunch time (Bijou, 1968). Data were taken on his eating and his out-of-seat behavior. Using bites of dessert as the reinforcing contingencies, the experimenter demonstrated that the child's eating problems could be eliminated.

SUMMARY AND CONCLUSION

Granted that the behavioral technology of teaching handicapped children is in its formative stage, enough has been accomplished to demonstrate that this technology has tremendous potential for helping these children acquire essential academic and social behavior. Based on principles derived from 45 years of laboratory research, the behavioral approach to special teaching will surely become increasingly effective as further advances emerge from basic and applied research.

We do not expect school administrators to model their special classes on the classes described here because the Laboratory classes have been designed primarily to facilitate research on the technology of special teaching. To gain acceptance and approval, the format of special classes in the public schools would have to vary in pupil composition, size, and curriculum in accordance with the policies of the various school boards. However, all the classes based on the research described here would have certain features in common: a motivational plan based on positive (extrinsic and intrinsic) reinforcers that are meaningful (functional) for each child; programmed instruction in reading, writing, arithmetic, language, and related subjects; and teachers skilled in arranging conditions so as to encourage academic and social learning. Such special classes would provide handicapped children with an educational environment not only conducive to good academic achievement but also pleasant and enjoyable.

The development of an effective technology of special teaching has far-reaching *implications* for education, especially for the training of teachers. Training potential teachers in the behavioral technology described here requires a college curriculum that has yet to be developed. Because the approach is derived from relatively new assumptions and conceptions about human development, learning, instruction, assessment, emotion, and motivation, any attempt to merge behavior analysis and applied behavioral analysis with subjects traditionally taught in teacher training courses would only dilute the potency of the technology. A thorough revision of the curriculum in teacher training is indicated.

Another implication of this approach relates to teaching personnel. Since this technology is based on individualized instruction, each child requires more time and attention than a teacher working alone can provide. As we have pointed out, an assistant is necessary to help prepare individual programs, conduct tutorials, and keep records. It is not necessary for the assistant to have a great deal of formal education. She may be a high school or college student, a parent, or a capable, retired man or woman.

A third implication is that special classes should be designed for and limited to kindergarten and primary-age children, to which they should be assigned as soon as their problems are identified. Special classes restricted to young children before they become "failures" serve both a remedial and preventative function.

The fourth implication, and the most important of all, bears on the necessity for individual instruction in all elementary grades. The gains a child makes in a special class cannot serve as a foundation for further academic achievement unless the programs in special and regular classes are interrelated in all essential details so that a child can smoothly and readily make the transition from special to regular class. Such meshing can be realized only if both types of classes are organized and operated on an individualized instructional basis such as is attempted in prescription teaching or the Individual Pupil Instructional plan. This is not an unrealistic suggestion. Several schools in this country already follow this plan, among them, the Prairie School in Urbana, Illinois.

ACKNOWLEDGMENT

Linda S. Berner, Janet C. Gilmore, Jeffrey A. Grimm, and Ely Rayek contributed to the preparation of this manuscript. Their assistance is greatly appreciated.

REFERENCES

Baldwin, A. L., Kalhorn, J., & Breese, F. H. The appraisal of parent behavior. *Psychological Monographs*, 1949, 63, (4, Whole No. 299).

Barker, R. G., & Wright, H. F. *Midwest and it's children: The psychological ecology of an American town.* New York: Harper, 1955.

Bijou, S. W. Experimental studies of child behavior, normal and deviant. In L. Krasner and L. P. Ullmann (Eds.), *Research in behavior modification.* New York: Holt, 1965.

Bijou, S. W. Functional analysis of retarded development. In N. Ellis (Ed.), *International review of research in mental retardation.* Vol. 1. New York: Academic Press, 1966. (a)

Bijou, S. W. Application of experimental analysis of behavior principles in teaching academic tool subjects to retarded children. In N. N. Haring and R. J. Whelan (Eds.), *The University of Kansas Symposium: The learning environment. Relationship to behavior modification and implications for special education.* Kansas Studies in Education. Lawrence, Kansas: Univ. of Kansas Publ., School of Education, 1966, 16, No. 2, pp. 16-23.   (b)

Bijou, S. W. *Research in remedial guidance of young retarded children with behavior problems which interfere with academic learning and adjustment.* Final Report

Project No. 5-0961, Grant No. OEG-32-23-1020-6002, U.S. Dept. of Health, Education, and Welfare, Office of Education, Bureau of Research, Washington, D.C., June, 1968.

Bijou, S. W., Birnbrauer, J. S., Kidder, J. D., & Tague, C. Programmed instruction as an approach to the teaching of reading, writing, and arithmetic to retarded children. *Psychological Record*, 1966, **16**, 505-522.

Bijou, S. W., Peterson, R. F., & Ault, M. A. A method to integrate descriptive and experimental field studies at the level of data and empirical concepts. *Journal of Applied Experimental Analysis*, 1968, **2**, 175-191.

Bijou, S. W., Peterson, R. F., Harris, F. R., Allen, K. E., & Johnston, M. S. Methodology for experimental studies of young children in natural settings. *Psychological Record*, 1969, **19**, 177-210.

Bijou, S. W., & Peterson, R. F. The psychological assessment of children: A functional analysis. In P. McReynolds (Ed.), *Advances in psychological assessment*. Vol. 2. Palo Alto, Calif.: Science & Behavior Books, 1971, pp. 63-78.

Birnbrauer, J. S., Kidder, J. D., & Tague, C. E. Programing reading from the teachers' point of view. *Programmed Instruction*, 1964, **3** (7), 1-2.

Birnbrauer, J. S., & Lawler, J. Token reinforcement for learning. *Mental Retardation*, 1964, **2**, 275-279.

Birnbrauer, J. S., Wolf, M. N., Kidder, J. D., & Tague, C. Classroom behavior of retarded pupils with token reinforcement. *Journal of Experimental Child Psychology*, 1965, **2**, 219-235.

Caldwell, B. *The preschool inventory*. Princeton, New Jersey: Educational Testing Service, 1967.

Dunn, L. M. *Peabody picture vocabulary test*. Minneapolis, Minnesota: American Guidance Service, 1959.

Hawkins, R. P., Peterson, R. F., Schweid, E., & Bijou, S. W. Behavior therapy in the home: Amelioration of problem parent-child relations with the parent in a therapeutic role. *Journal of Experimental Child Psychology*, 1966, **4**, 99-107.

Jastak, J. F., Bijou, S. W., & Jastak, S. R. *Wide range achievement test*. (Rev. ed.) Wilmington, Delaware: Guidance Associates, 1965.

Johnson, G. O. Special education for the mentally handicapped—A paradox. *Exceptional Children*, 1962, **29**, 62-69.

Peterson, R. F., Cox, M. A., & Bijou, S. W. Training children to work productively in classroom groups. *Exceptional Children*, 1971, **37**, 491-500.

Risley, T. R., & Wolf, M. M. Experimental manipulation of autistic behaviors and generalization into the home. In S. W. Bijou and D. M. Baer (Eds.), *Child development: Readings in experimental analysis*. New York: Appleton, 1967.

Sajwaj, T. E., Twardosz, S., Kantor, N., & Burke, M. Side-effects of extinction procedures in a remedial preschool. Unpublished manuscript, Univ. of Illinois, 1970.

Skinner, B. F. *The technology of teaching*. New York: Appleton, 1968.

Sloane, H. N., Johnston, M. G., & Bijou, S. W. Successive modification of aggressive behavior and aggressive fantasy play by management of contingencies. *Journal of Child Psychology and Psychiatry*, 1967, **8**, 217-226.

Sloane, H. N., Jr., & MacAulay, B. D. (Eds.) *Operant procedures in remedial speech and language training*. Boston, Massachusetts: Houghton, 1968.

Wolf, M. M., Risley, T., & Mees, H. Application of operant conditioning procedures to the behavior problems of an autistic child. *Behaviour Research and Therapy*, 1964, **1**, 305-312.

Discussion: Implementation of Operant Procedures for the Treatment of Handicapped Children

FLORENTE LOPEZ R.

Bijou's contribution to the research and treatment of behavior problems and behavioral deficits in children may be summarized as follows.

1. His influence through the functional analysis of three related problems: mental retardation, child development, and intelligence (Bijou, 1963; Bijou, 1968a; and Bijou, 1971). From these analyses, a new concept of mental retardation has been derived in which the behavioral deficits are considered as a function of biological, physical, and social variables.

2. His interest in the development and integration of a methodology for the experimental analysis of child behavior and development both in the laboratory and in the natural environment (Bijou & Baer, 1966; Bijou, Peterson, & Ault, 1968; Bijou, Peterson, Harris, Allen, & Johnston, 1969; Bijou & Peterson, 1971).

3. His influence in the development of a technology for special education (among others, Bijou, 1968b; Bijou, 1969; Bijou, 1970).

Bijou's chapter is more representative of the third of these points. However, it necessarily implies his philosophy about the functional analysis of retarded behavior as well as the methods for experimental analysis of behavior. The present paper does not pretend to be an evaluation of Bijou's work but a brief analysis of (1) some of the problems encountered in trying to apply the experimental and theoretical principles to solve behavior problems and establish behavior repertoires in retarded children and (2) some of the difficulties in adapting those techniques to Latin-American institutions dealing with the same type of problems.

THE CENTER FOR TRAINING AND SPECIAL EDUCATION (CTSE)

The present paper represents a good opportunity to acknowledge Bijou's influence on the development of behavior modification programs in the Department of Psychology at the University of Veracruz in Xalapa and, especially, his efforts in the establishment of the CTSE, the first Mexican institution devoted to the treatment of retarded children through the use of operant procedures.

Even though behavior modification principles and procedures were known in Mexico, they were not applied practically until 1967. At that time Bijou, visiting the Department of Psychology at the University of Veracruz, gave a general explanation of the programs he was developing and pointed out how similar programs could be put into effect in Mexico. A year later, the department initiated a demonstration program on behavior modification with a group of six retarded children whose behavioral deficits and problems were so severe that the School of Special Education at Xalapa considered it valuable to try new procedures for their treatment. The initial results could not have been more rewarding. The program was expanded and became the CTSE, which now offers its services to about 40 children.

The reasons for an institution of this kind were probably similar to the reasons expressed by Bijou when he described admission practices and commented on the results obtained in special classes for the mentally retarded in the United States. Perhaps we should add that the only provisions for the retarded in Mexico have heretofore been as follows. (1) With the severely retarded, provision of medical services only, dealing mainly with the satisfaction of the patients' basic needs, both state and private institutions having abandoned almost every other type of treatment. (2) With the mildly retarded, the utilization of the same teaching techniques as those provided for the education of the normal child, the only difference being that the handicapped were taught at a slower rate. This was probably due to the belief that the retarded child does not "assimilate" at the same speed as the normal child.

The CTSE can be considered a modest Mexican replication of the programs already developed by Bijou, first, at the Rainier School in Washington, where it was shown that institutionalized retarded children could be better trained with techniques based on an experimental analysis of behavior and, second, at the Child Behavior Laboratory of the University of Illinois, where a research demonstration program applied remedial education and training techniques to the rehabilitation of young problem children.

The goals of the working program of the CTSE have basically been those described by Bijou (1968b), which aim to develop social and verbal behaviors and to promote academic repertoires, mainly writing and reading. Likewise, a token economy along with social reinforcement has been used as a motivational system.

The basic and most challenging problem confronting us has been that of generalization of the behavior established in the treatment environment to the natural environment. Initial attempts in dealing with this problem led us to consider generalization in relation to three particular points: (1) What behaviors are considered to be important for community living?; (2) What is the best motivational system for the establishment of these behavior repertoires?; and (3) What is the importance of the similarity between the treatment setting and the natural environment? In other words, a program can be successful in establishing behavior, but if those behaviors are not reinforced by the community, generalization cannot be expected. Similarly, a motivational system may be successful in establishing a behavioral repertoire, but if the normal social reinforcers are not functional for the individual, no generalization may be forthcoming. Finally, generalization may also depend on the similarity between the treatment setting and the community where the individual will live.

A radical alternative to avoid the generalization problem might be to develop closed therapeutic communities based on a behavioral technology and architecture in such a way as to establish behavioral repertoires suited for an adjusted life within that community. However, this possibility is not yet realistic for underdeveloped or, for that matter, for developed countries.

A second possibility might be to make a descriptive and experimental analysis of the necessary conditions for the occurrence of established behaviors in the treatment setting and, by means of the reinforcement practices of the social group and its special programs, for their maintenance. We believe that this statement can be better discussed in regard to the three aspects related to the generalization problem.

Based on the previous assumptions, the first decision to be made is what behaviors we wish to establish in the child. This decision, it seems to us, must be made on the basis of a social criterion; that is, the behaviors chosen as targets should be those that are not only of practical use in the natural environment but are usually maintained by social reinforcement practices. In this regard, we would like to discuss two classes of behaviors that we consider important in the acquisition of behavioral repertoires: imitation and instructional control.

The establishment of a generalized imitative repertoire (Baer & Sherman, 1964; Metz, 1965) would be utilized as a teaching technique, shortening the often long process of shaping in the establishment of new behaviors (Peterson, 1968). Imitation, as a behavior modification procedure, has been utilized mainly in the establishment of verbal behavior (e.g., Lovaas, Barberich, Perloff, & Schaffer. 1966). However, other applications might also be explored. such as (1) the role of imitation in the establishment of social and vocational repertoires in children with behavioral deficits and (2) imitation as a useful procedure in the establishment of behavior under instructional control. After a basic imitative repertoire has been established, the experimenter may instruct the child to do a specific task at the same time that he is modeling the behavior to be established under instructional control. Once the child is imitating the stimuli presented by the model under those conditions, such stimuli can be faded out and finally leave control under instructions alone.

Instructional control, along with imitation, is probably the most frequently utilized technique in the education of children in the home as well as in educational settings. Once the behavior of a subject is under instructional control, its use may offer a greater versatility than imitation since it is possible to establish behavior repertoires (or, at least, to put them under discriminative control) of a greater complexity. Unfortunately, as far as we know, an experimental analysis of following-instructions behavior remains to be done. Perhaps a first step could be to investigate whether the generalized imitation phenomenon is, in fact, a more general phenomenon also observed in other behaviors among which following-instructions behavior is found. That is, one could ask whether it is possible to establish a response class of following instructions in which a group of instructions is reinforced, this having the effect of increasing the probability of following another set of instructions that have never been reinforced. Thus, the necessity of shaping or modeling this second group of responses would be eliminated.

The second point in the analysis of generalization is the selection of a motivational system. The motivational system employed in the training of retarded children has usually been the establishment of a generalized reinforcer, as in the token economy. In some cases, provisions are made so that the control exerted by the generalized reinforcer can be transferred to social reinforcement systems. In this way, it is supposed that children's behavior will not only be under the control of the contrived reinforcers dispensed in the treatment setting but that the behavior will be controlled by the reinforcers normally dispensed in the social group. Combining the previous procedures with the training of parents in contingency management could result in an increased effectiveness of the programs.

It may be interesting to study another type of generalized reinforcer that might be useful in these settings: money reinforcement, since money is certainly used to maintain a considerable amount of behavior in the social environment. However, it should be pointed out that the problem is not only to establish money as a generalized reinforcer but also to analyze the schedules in which money is usually dispensed in society, since the requirements are usually high, and straining may result as a consequence of the requirements. The establishment of social events and money as reinforcers might well expedite the development of intervention programs in several settings, such as the home, the school, or the sheltered workshop, under appropriate reinforcement schedules.

Finally, there is the problem of the treatment setting versus the natural environment. Often, those behaviors established in a particular setting remain functional only under the discriminative control of that setting. Thus, if we are trying to extend the control from the treatment setting to some other setting, provisions should be made to ensure this extension. One possibility is to include the reinforcement contingencies in the new setting. In order to do so, it will be necessary to implement observation procedures in the natural environment and to train nonprofessionals, a subject already discussed in other papers presented in this volume.

SOME SUGGESTIONS FOR THE IMPLEMENTATION OF REHABILITATION PROGRAMS IN LATIN AMERICA

Although the implementation of behavior modification techniques for the treatment of retarded children is relatively inexpensive, financial support may represent a problem in the Latin countries and, specifically, in Mexico. The general policy has been to provide minimal financial support (if any at all) for educating the retarded; most of the funds are allocated to elementary school education. It appears that there is a kind of rejection of paying for the education of those who are not likely to contribute to the society. Consequently, we anticipate that there will be an emphasis on the development of low-cost programs. The following are some suggestions for the most profitable utilization of whatever funds become available.

1. Behavior modification programs applied to rehabilitation problems have demonstrated that it is essential to establish vocational repertoires in the handicapped. Only in this way can we increase the probability of the social reintegration of not only the retarded but various other groups of handicapped. Crosson (1969), Hunt and Zimmerman (1969), and Zimmerman, Stuckey Garlick, and Miller (1969) have shown that it is possible to establish and maintain working behavior in individuals with behavioral deficits through operant procedures. In the Latin-American countries, the teaching of such vocational repertoires could readily lead to the establishment of sheltered workshops where the earnings could be used to develop and maintain a center for the clients' own treatment, if needed, and for their further education, academic or social.

2. Operant techniques have been successfully utilized in the establishment or maintenance of social behavior repertoires in several different settings: Burchard (1967), Phillips (1968), and Cohen, Filipczak, and Bis (1965) in institutions for antisocial adolescents and Ayllon and Azrin (1968) in hospitals with psychiatric patients. Lindsley (1964) pointed out that it is possible to avoid behavioral deterioration in the aged through the establishment of a controlled environment and prosthetic instruments and that the implementation of a generalized reinforcer may set the occasion for an optimum behavior repertoire. Perhaps it would be possible to implement conjoint programs for the treatment of retardates and individuals with other types of problems (psychiatric patients, the aged, etc.) by assigning the patients to groups according to the similarity of their deficits. Thus, patients with minor deficits could be taught certain behavior repertoires that would enable them to function as aides in the programming or training of individuals with more severe deficits (Lindsley, 1964). This would

result in a substantial saving of money for, as Bijou has pointed out, although an operant technology is based primarily on individualized instruction, it is totally unnecessary for all the personnel to be professionally educated.

3. Some children attending schools of special education who do not present serious problems that require a direct intervention in their own environment could be handled as outpatients. In such cases, the problem is to find an economical way of dealing with each child in his home or school. Hawkins, Peterson, Schweid and Bijou (1966), among others, have shown that it is possible to deal with infant behavior problems using the parents as therapeutic agents and that this can be accomplished in the home. And other procedures are under investigation in which personnel requirements are kept at a minimum. Cantrell, Cantrell, Huddleston, and Woolridge (1969) have adapted operant procedures in making behavioral contracts with parents in which the contingencies are specified and the parents are responsible for carrying them out. One of the difficulties with this kind of procedure is that it requires the cooperation of the persons administering the contingencies. In an attempt to minimize this problem, Tharp and Wetzel (1969) have designed a procedure that analyzes both the consequences maintaining the behavior of the manager of the contingencies and the consequences potentially effective in modifying the child's behavior. Their results seem encouraging.

CONCLUSIONS

The title of Bijou's chapter clearly describes the objectives of his work as well as that of other investigators dealing with handicapped children: the development of a technology for special education. In this regard, Bijou's contribution has been not only the development of specific techniques, but also the integration, analysis, and application of different operant procedures to what we may consider the basic educational unit: the classroom. Our intention has been only to point out some of the problems faced in attempting to adapt those techniques to environments having different features from those in which they were initially studied and developed. Nevertheless, our final comment is that in order for the necessary adaptations to be effective they must faithfully adhere to the very same principles and technology of special education. Compromises and deviations will serve only to delay progress in this field.

REFERENCES

Ayllon, T., & Azrin, N. *The token economy: A motivational system for therapy and rehabilitation.* New York: Appleton, 1968.

Baer, D. M., & Sherman, J. A. Reinforcement control of generalized imitation in young children. *Journal of Experimental Child Psychology,* 1964, 1, 37-49.

Bijou, S. W. Theory and research in mental (developmental) retardation. *Psychological Record,* 1963, 13, 95-110.

Bijou, S. W. Child behavior and development: A behavioral analysis. *International Journal of Psychology,* 1968, 3, 221-238.   (a)

Bijou, S. W. Research in remedial guidance of young retarded children with behavior problems which interfere with academic learning and adjustment. Final Report Project No. 5-0961. U.S. Department of Health, Education, and Welfare, June 1968. (b)

Bijou, S. W. Promoting optimum learning in children. In P. Wolf and R. MacKeith (Eds.), *Planning for better learning*. London: Spastics International Medical Publ., 1969. Pp. 58-67.

Bijou, S. W. A behavioral analysis of teaching and special education. Unpublished manuscript, Univ. of Illinois, 1970.

Bijou, S. W. Environment and intelligence: A behavioral analysis. In R. Cancro (Ed.), *Contributions to intelligence*. New York: Grune & Stratton, 1971. Pp. 221-239.

Bijou, S. W., & Baer, D. M. Operant methods in child behavior and development. In W. K. Honig (Ed.), *Operant behavior: Areas of research and application*. New York: Appleton, 1966.

Bijou, S. W., Peterson, R. F., & Ault, M. A. A method to integrate descriptive and experimental field studies at the level of data and empirical concepts. *Journal of Applied Behavior Analysis*, 1968, 1, 175-191.

Bijou, S. W., Peterson, R. F., Harris, F. R., Allen, K. E., & Johnston, M. S. Methodology for experimental studies of young children in natural settings. *Psychological Record*, 1969, 19, 177-210.

Bijou, S. W., & Peterson, R. F. Psychological assessment in children: A functional analysis. In P. McReynolds (Ed.), *Advances in psychological assessment*. Vol. 2. Palo Alto, California: Science & Behavior Books, 1971. Pp. 63-78.

Burchard, J. D. Systematic socialization: A programmed environment for the rehabilitation of antisocial retardates. *Psychological Record*, 1967, 17, 461-476.

Cantrell, R. P., Cantrell, R. M., Huddleston, C. M., & Woolridge, R. C. Contingency contracting with school problems. *Journal of Applied Behavior Analysis*, 1969, 2, 215-220.

Cohen, H. L., Filipczak, J. A., & Bis, J. S. Case project: Contingencies application for special education. Progress Report, U.S. Department of Health, Education, and Welfare, 1965.

Crosson, J. E. A technique for programming sheltered workshop environments for training severely retarded workers. *American Journal of Mental Deficiency*, 1969, 73, 814-818.

Hawkins, R. P., Peterson, R. F., Schweid, E., & Bijou, S. W. Behavior therapy in the home: Amelioration of problem parent-child relations with the parent in a therapeutic role. *Journal of Experimental Child Psychology*, 1966, 4, 99-107.

Hunt, J. G., & Zimmerman, J. Stimulating productivity in a simulated sheltered workshop setting. *American Journal of Mental Deficiency*, 1969, 74, 43-49.

Lindsley, O. R. Geriatric behavioral prosthetics. In R. Kastembaum (Ed.), *New thoughts on old age*. New York: Springer Publ., 1964.

Lovaas, O. I., Barberich, J. P., Perloff, B. F., & Schaffer, B. Acquisition of imitative speech in schizophrenic children. *Science*, 1966, 151, 705-707.

Metz, J. R. Conditioning generalized imitation in autistic children. *Journal of Experimental Child Psychology*, 1965, 2, 389-399.

Peterson, R. F. Imitation: A basic behavioral mechanism. In H. N. Sloane and B. D. McAulay (Eds.), *Operant procedures in remedial speech and language training*. Boston, Massachusetts: Houghton, 1968.

Phillips, E. L. Achievement place: Token reinforcement procedures in a home-style rehabilitation setting for pre-delinquent boys. *Journal of Applied Behavior Analysis*, 1968, 1, 213-223.

Tharp, R. G., & Wetzel, R. J. *Behavior modification in the natural environment*. New York: Academic Press, 1969.

Zimmerman, J., Stuckey, T. E., Garlick, B. J., & Miller, M. Effects of token reinforcement in multiply handicapped clients in a sheltered workshop. *Rehabilitation Literature*, 1969 30, 34-41.

The Teaching Family: A New Model for the Treatment of Deviant Child Behavior in the Community[1]

MONTROSE M. WOLF, ELERY L. PHILLIPS, AND DEAN L. FIXSEN

The failure of institutional treatment programs to help deviant children as well as the inhumane and debilitating conditions of institutions for children has been clearly documented by many authors such as Stuart (1970), Goffman (1961), and Wolfensberger (1970). These authorities and others have indicated that the treatment programs in institutions for delinquent, psychotic, and retarded children are not preparing these children for community life. Instead, these children seemingly are being taught passive-dependent behavior that is appropriate for the institutional inmate but which is contrary in most respects to the requirements of community living (Ullman & Krasner, 1965; Stuart, 1970; Goffman, 1961).

If the goals of the treatment programs of our institutions are to teach a child to become a successful member of his community, then the treatment program must teach him to live in a bisexual world, to acquire the social skills necessary for family and community life, to achieve the vocational and academic

[1]This research was supported by Public Health Service grant MH 16609 from NIMH (the Center of Studies of Crime and Delinquency) and NICHD grant HD 03144 to the Bureau of Child Research and the Department of Human Development, University of Kansas.

requirements for employment, to learn to work for money, and to spend or save money for his needs. Almost none of these skills can be taught in a custodial institution. In an institution, the child is usually segregated on the basis of sex, taught dependency on a hospital-like routine, given little work that would transfer as a useful skill to the outside community, and taught to live on the "welfare system" of the institution rather than to learn to be as responsible as possible for his own needs.

Much of this undesirable outcome may be due to the fact that most institutional treatment programs are based on the illness model of deviant behavior. The usefulness of the illness model of treatment recently has come into question. If these children were ill, it might be reasonable to place them in large hospital-like institutions and to have their basic needs administered to by "attendant" personnel, who might be able to provide adequate custodial care but who are often too undertrained and overworked to serve as teachers and models of the complex skills that must be taught for successful community life.

The illness model of deviant behavior with its hospital-like, institutional treatment philosophy is becoming less generally accepted because of its history of repeated failure and great expense. The credibility of the mental illness model is also lessened as the relationship between learning variables and deviant behavior becomes better understood. Instead of basing our treatment strategies on a *mental illness model,* modern behavior theory suggests a *behavior deficiency model* of deviant behavior where the behavior problems of children are viewed as deficiencies in essential skills. These behavioral deficits are considered a result of inadequate histories of reinforcement and instruction rather than as due to some hypothetical internal psychopathology. Accordingly, treatment programs based on the behavior deficiency model are designed to establish the important behavioral competencies that the child has not learned. In contrast, treatment strategies based on the mental illness model view behavioral deficiencies as superficial and unimportant symptoms and attempt instead to cure the "underlying mental disease."

This increasing interest in treatment programs based on the behavior deficiency model is occuring concurrently with a second important trend in the treatment of child behavior problems. There is now a worldwide trend away from institutional programs, because community-based treatment of deviant child behavior seems to be more effective, cheaper, and more humane than the institutionalization of children. This trend has been particularly evident in Scandinavia where Denmark and Sweden now support, with government funds, programs for almost all deviant and retarded children in their communities. Several states in the United States also have recently introduced financial incentives for communities to provide community-based services for their deviant children rather than depend upon state institutional treatment programs. As a result many states are reporting substantial decreases in their institutionalization rates for delinquent, retarded, and psychotic children. In some states the reduction in the institutionalization of children has been spectacular. For example, about three years ago, California introduced an incentive program that pays up to $4000 to a community for each child who was eligible for institutionalization but who was not placed in a state reformatory, and there has been a reduction by one-third in the delinquent children sent to California reformatories. The state of Washington has recently implemented a similar program, and the results have been equally dramatic. Washington State reformatories are now approximately one-third empty, and two state institutions have been closed.

The success of the community programs for the retarded is even more dramatic in some states. The recent President's Committee on Mental Retardation ("Residential Services for the Mentally Retarded," U.S. Government Printing Office, Washington, D.C., 1970) compared the "dehumanizing custodial care" of the mentally retarded with the treatment of prisoners of war. Their recommendation was to "normalize" the lives of the retarded: to take them out of the institutions and to integrate them into the community. This recommendation is being implemented in several states.

The new emphasis away from building institutions and toward developing community-based treatment programs was reaffirmed recently at the 1970 White House Conference on Children, which gave it one of the highest priorities. As a result of these trends we are quite possibly on the verge of a new era of the treatment of deviant children. One result, it is hoped, will be experimentation with a wide variety of treatment models that are compared and evaluated in terms of effectiveness and cost.

Many programs will undoubtedly focus on training parents and potential parents in child behavior shaping and management procedures. Authorities agree that most of the deviant child's behavior problems might be prevented or overcome if their parents had better child management skills. Unfortunately, however, there are many parents who have such severe personal problems that a routine parent training program may have little effect. These parents will need more intensive help. Thus, rather than relying on these parents to teach their severely deviant children all of the complex social, prevocational, and self-care skills that they need, it may be necessary to provide special training programs in the community that will have this educational responsibility. If the child's behavioral deficiencies can be modified in a special training program, the parents may be able to learn to *maintain* the appropriate behavior even though they were not able to *establish* it originally without the help of the special training program.

In Kansas we are currently developing a model program that we believe could fulfill these special training functions. We refer to our model as the *teaching-family*. We envision placement of children and adolescents with severe behavior problems in family-styled settings in their communities. Six to ten children would participate in each family-style home. Each teaching-family program would be administered by a couple that we refer to as *teaching-parents*. The title teaching-parents is given to distinguish them from the more traditional, untrained custodial house-parents or foster-parents. In our model the teaching-parents are given a year's professional training. Also, they are paid a professional salary at the level of public school teachers, since they are teachers in the fullest sense. They have the explicit responsibility to teach the social skills, self-care skills, vocational skills, and academic skills that are necessary to make these deviant youths successful citizens in their community. The specific behavioral goals can be determined by each community or neighborhood. In this way each program can reflect the unique characteristics and customs of the local citizens.

In Kansas, we have been involved in establishing some teaching-family programs designed to help youths who have been described as delinquent or in danger of becoming delinquent. Currently we are connected with four teaching-family homes that are in various stages of development. These programs are based on Achievement Place, a teaching-family program that is completing its fourth year of operation (Phillips, 1968). The behavior modification system at Achievement Place is designed to provide a maximum amount of feedback to the youths when they first enter the program. Each new boy begins on a token economy where his behavior each day determines the number of tokens (or points) that he will have to earn to buy the reinforcers (privileges) for the next day. The back-up reinforcers are all privileges and items that are naturally available in the home. Thus, the reinforcement system adds nothing to the cost of the program. As a boy develops the target skills, the immediate concrete reinforcement is gradually replaced by a more remote, ambiguous, and, we think, natural set of feedback conditions. As the boy accomplishes the behavioral goals of the program, he and his parents are prepared for the youth's return to his natural home. The preliminary results of the Achievement Place program indicate that it is effective in correcting a number of social, self-care, and academic behavior problems and that the youths are progressing better than a small sample of comparable deviant youths who also have come into repeated contact with the police and the court and have been placed on probation or sent to the state reformatory.

Successful dissemination of the Achievement Place teaching-family model will have at least two facets. (1) We must continue to develop practical and effective behavior modification procedures and to evaluate them in a convincing manner, and (2) we must be able to train new teaching-parents to apply these procedures successfully.

The attempt to develop practical and effective treatment procedures is a continuous informal process at Achievement Place. Once we suspect that a procedure may be effective, based on our informal observations, we arrange to evaluate it formally. Evidence has been published demonstrating the effectiveness of the Achievement Place token economy in modifying aggressive speech, poor grammar, promptness, homework preparation, and room cleaning and other household maintenance behaviors (Phillips, 1968). More recently, we have completed the development and evaluation of a procedure for modifying the disruptive and attentive public school classroom behavior of the youths. We will present a detailed description of this research as an example of our general research methodology.

Most of the boys who have come into Achievement Place either have been expelled from school or were in immediate danger of being expelled from school. It quickly became evident that we had to find a practical and effective technique to deal with the disruptive behavior problems of the boys in their classroom. We also discovered that the teachers of these boys were not very eager to apply positive social reinforcement for small approximations to appropriate behavior or to spend time administering token reinforcement for improvement in classroom behavior. It was clear that a practical system would have to involve almost no teacher training, time, or effort. Fortunately, systematic research has produced a simple, practical, and yet effective technique (Bailey, Wolf, & Phillips, 1970). The method did not require precise and continuous data collection or administration of tokens or attention from the teacher. In fact, the only requirement was that the teacher make a few dichotomous decisions at the end of the class period about the behavior of the boy in class. (1) Did the youth follow the teacher's rules today? (2) Did the youth make good use of his class time? (3) Did the youth complete his assignment at an acceptable level of accuracy?

The teaching-parents applied the procedures as follows. The youth was instructed to take a behavior report card to class each day for the teacher to mark as described. Then the youth took the card home to the teaching-parents. If the youth's card had been marked "yes" by every teacher in every category, then the child earned a number of points and privileges. If the child was checked "no" in any category, he lost a predetermined number of points.

We evaluated a prototype of the procedure in a summer school program that was attended by five of the boys then in Achievement Place. The boys went to a special classroom setting and worked in math books in a classroom that was much like a regular school classroom with desks, blackboard, pictures on the walls, and a teacher whose role it was to answer questions and grade problems. In addition, an observation booth adjoined the classroom from which observers recorded whether the boys were working in their workbooks or were being disruptive and inattentive (according to a set of detailed and reliable response definitions).

As shown in Fig. 1, during the first three days of the summer school the boys were perfect students, working diligently and not talking out or daydreaming. Then they began to "test" the teacher. In a few more days they became less attentive and more disruptive, exhibiting the same behavior we had observed in their public school classrooms. In fact, they spent about 65% of their time talking, getting out of their seats, looking out the window, and throwing their pencils and only about 35% of their time attending to the study materials.

In the next step of the experiment, the boys were required by the teaching-parents to carry the daily behavior report card. The boys were told that the teacher would check "yes" or "no," depending upon whether the boy had "studied the whole period" and "obeyed the rules." If a boy got all "yeses," he was assured of several privileges that day; on the other hand, if a boy got a "no," he would lose a significant number of points and, thus, privileges unless he earned additional points in other ways.

Under the first condition, our special classroom teacher was instructed to give "yeses" regardless of what the boys did in the classroom. During this "yes" only condition, the study behavior initially increased, and the rule violation behavior initially decreased. But over the next several days inappropriate classroom behavior returned to a high level. At this point, the teacher was instructed to give "yeses" only when a boy had behaved appropriately in the classroom.

In order to assure precision in the teacher's marking the cards, the observer in the booth assigned the report card grades on the basis of the observational data. A 10% level of each behavior was set. That is, more than 10% nonstudy or rule violation behavior led to a boy's card being checked "no." Each boy received a "no" the first day of this new condition and lost points when he returned to Achievement Place. There was an immediate improvement in the study behavior and a reduction in the rule violation behavior of the boys. Soon they each studied and obeyed the rules better than 90% of the time. After two weeks of this high level of appropriate behavior, the teaching-parents announced to the boys that they would not have to bring the notes from school to earn their privileges each day. After three days under this no back-up condition, the boys were at almost a 50% level of disruptive behavior and had declined to approximately 25% study behavior. When the teaching-parents again announced that each boy was expected to bring the card home each day, excellent classroom behavior emerged once more and remained at better than 90% during the remainder of the study. These data from the group of five boys showed clear effects of the daily behavior report card procedure. Each of the five boys as individuals showed almost exactly the same effects that you see in the grouped data (Fig. 1).

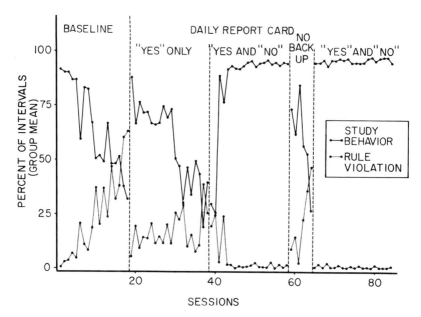

Fig. 1. Mean percent of intervals of study and rule violation for all five subjects under each treatment condition (From Bailey, Wolf, and Phillips, 1970).

The daily behavior report card procedure with the back-up reinforcement in the home has now been applied to a number of boys in their regular public school classrooms. In each case the teacher simply decides at the end of the day whether the boy has followed her rules and studied and performed at her level of expectation. These decisions require very little time on her part. In approximately 75% of the cases, we have found immediate and dramatic improvements in these behaviors. In those instances where the procedure did not work, it appears as though the teacher had not developed explicit rules in her classroom or she did not differentiate appropriate and inappropriate behavior on the part of the youths. Adaptation of the daily behavior report card procedure so that it is effective with such teachers remains to be accomplished. Nevertheless, in most cases the daily behavior report card with the back-up home reinforcement seems to be a very effective and practical procedure for the teaching-parents to gain rapid control over the behavior of a youth who is about to be expelled from school. Research is now being conducted using a similar procedure to effect academic achievement. On the average, we have found that Achievement Place youths increase their report card grades from something less than a D average to approximately a C average. We have not yet analyzed exactly what components of the program, i.e., the daily behavior report card system, the home tutoring program, the points for improved report card grades, etc., have been responsible for this improvement.

A similar remote reinforcement procedure has also been adapted in the training program for parents. We have found that by establishing important skills at Achievement Place and then providing the boys the motivation in the form of the daily behavior report card it seems that rapid control also can be gained over many problem behaviors in the home.

Some of the procedures are not so well established and evaluated as the remote reinforcement card. One of the most fascinating investigations now underway concerns the peer group phenomena that emerge in the teaching-family program. The influence of the peer group on the delinquent has been clearly described by a number of investigators (Cohn, 1955; Shaw & McKay, 1942; Thrasher, 1939). These authorities have also indicated that much peer group pressure is for antisocial behavior. It is easy to see how a similar antisocial gang could develop in a teaching-family setting. By associating the adults exclusively with aversive control, by allowing the gang members to cover up for one another, by making extensive use of group consequences so that the youths suffer for one another's inappropriate behavior, and by having many seemingly arbitrary rules and "unfair" sanctions, one could probably manage to align all of the youths against the adults rather easily. Many authorities on institutional programs for youths have reported instances of counter control in their institutions. On the other hand, there are a number of procedures that might be useful in promoting active cooperation between the youths and the adults. With these procedures the teaching-parents might be able to arrange peer group contingencies for appropriate behavior and peer group sanctions for inappropriate behavior that would promote the goals of the teaching-family rather than the other way around.

We are currently investigating a method involving the peer group that seems to be effective in controlling inappropriate behavior; it seems to be beneficial to the boys and to be preferred by them. It involves the teaching-parents establishing a democratic semi-self-governing system in the home. Of course, the adults must retain final authority, but they can introduce a degree of self-government so that the program will respond to the preferences of the youths. Semi-self-governing youth programs have previously been described by others such as Neil (1960) at Summerhill and Makarenko (1953) at the Gorkey Colony, a program for delinquent youth in Russia. Unfortunately, several serious attempts to establish similar self-governing programs based on the work of Neil and Makarenko have not met with much success. Apparently, systematic research will be necessary to develop a replicable system.

It seems to us that there are four behaviors that the teaching-parents need to shape and to reinforce in order for a semi-self-governing system to function. The boys must learn to set behavioral rules, to report violations of these rules, to decide about guilt, and to assign consequences for violation of the rules.

There are certain rules that *must* be set and enforced. These are defined by the law and the community. For example, it is not possible to allow severe physical abuse of either boys or teaching-parents. However, there are a number of steps between simple physical contact and actual physical abuse. Contact sports, such as basketball and football, are one step. Boxing with boxing gloves is another step; simple fist fights of short duration is at still another step below the point of actual severe physical abuse. The boys themselves could help decide what the rules should be regarding each of these steps. As it turns out, the boys at Achievement Place have voted to have very strict rules to control fighting and painful physical contact. Given an effective self-governing mechanism, the boys' preference seems to be to eliminate all painful physical contact. This decision has required the boys to develop detailed rules about physical abuse, report such instances, decide on guilt, and levy sanctions against one another.

While it may be necessary, initially, to have extrinsic reinforcement contingencies for engaging in rule-setting behavior in the group meetings (or "trials" as these meetings are referred to by the boys), it appears as though the rule-setting behavior very quickly comes under the control of the natural consequences of having an orderly society. The boys soon begin assuming responsibility for the rules in all areas of their lives. The obvious benefits to them are clear. They are able to avoid the domination by physical strength that is often the basis for rule-setting in a delinquent gang. They also make rules against intimidation and threats among peer group members. The teaching-parents provide the initial reinforcement of rule-setting behavior and also play an important role in providing the boys with examples of rules that the boys may wish to adopt and in discussing the possible consequences for each of the rules. The advice and guidance of the teaching-parents is essential since these boys have had little practice in democratic social processes.

The second important behavior is the reporting of rule violations. Since reports by the peers are the only means of gathering much of the data that is essential for the semi-self-governing process, the reporting behavior is critical to its success. Reporting of rule violations also is probably the most difficult behavior to foster since reporting behavior in the past has frequently been punished by peers and seems to resemble the behavior of "informers," "stool-pigeons," and "rat finks." The importance of reporting behavior for their present semi-self-governing system can be explained to the boys, and the differences in the present system and the behavior of informers, etc., can be described. Analogies to their interests can be drawn. It can be explained, for example, that if someone were to steal their TV set and if they lived in a social group that has decided on a rule against stealing TV sets, then it would be very reasonable to report the theft of the TV set to the person in the social group who had the responsibility of enforcing that rule. Similarly, if they see their neighbor's TV set being stolen, then they have a responsibility to report the theft of their neighbor's TV set. Since the rule being broken is a rule they have agreed upon with their neighbor and want applied to their own TV set, it is easy to point out how it is in their best interest to take an active part in enforcing the rule. Because the teaching-parents have explained democratic procedures and set up extrinsic reinforcement for reporting behavior, it is possible to establish a high level of reporting behavior that seems to be consistent with the level of rule violation. At Achievement Place, for example, there are usually a couple of rule violations reported by the boys each day. One possible undesirable side effect of the reinforcement of reporting rule violations is that one might establish high rates of irrelevant tattling or complaining. But a rule against such tattling also can easily be established, and consequences applied.

The remaining important behavioral components for semi-self-government in the teaching-family are the decisions about guilt and the setting of sanctions. It would seem essential to have the boys participate in decisions about a peer's guilt and to mediate the sanctions for one another's rule infractions rather than to have the adults make all these decisions and decide upon all the consequences. Once a rule has been established, and it has been reported to be violated, the boys meet and have a "trial." First, they establish, to their satisfaction, the guilt or innocence of the accused and then decide upon the consequences, if guilt is established. The fact that the boys, rather than the teaching-parents, levy the consequences means that the teaching-parents are not directly paired with the penalties. It is not the boys against the teaching-parents; it is the boys largely governing themselves. The teaching-parents here, however, play a very important role. The boys are inexperienced in setting appropriate consequences. Frequently, the boys will levy overly harsh aversive consequences such as suggesting that a peer should have to wash the dinner dishes for six months as punishment for a minor offense. When this happens the teaching-parents suggest more moderate alternatives and present a case for what seem to be more appropriate consequences. Usually the boys reconsider and accept the more moderate consequences. The teaching-parents enjoy the role of moderator rather than disciplinarian.

There are possible difficulties in such a semi-self-governing system. For example, some of the stronger boys may very well attempt to take advantage of the system and try to intimidate other boys not to report a rule violation. If this occurs and if the smaller boy does report the rule violation as well as the intimidation threat, while the larger boy denies both, and there happens to be no further evidence or no witnesses, then the decision guilty or not guilty may be held in abeyance. Meanwhile, if the larger boy attempts to intimidate a second boy, who then reports the intimidation and rule violation, there would then be evidence from more than one boy that intimidation is taking place. It can then be up to the accused boy to prove his innocence. In other words, intimidation may take place but it can only take place to a very limited extent without evidence accumulating against the intimidator.

A second possible difficulty with the semi-self-governing system is that individuals may lie about the occurrence of rule violations. That is, they may report offenses that do not take place in order to acquire the token reinforcement for reporting behavior. Again, the system has a built-in correction procedure. If a boy accuses more than one of his peers of offenses that didn't take place he then has two accusors for lying. Again, the peer group majority decides whether the boy is guilty of lying, and he, in all likelihood, would be fined unless he could prove his innocence. Thus, while physical intimidation and lying about rule violations may occur in the system, they cannot occur frequently or the peers will levy consequences against the offenders.

A third problem with this system is that it does not seem to be very rewarding to most of the new boys. Usually the boys have been used to the gang style self-government where most decisions are made by the strongest and the most aggressive boys in their peer group. It appears that the new boys have to learn through experience the advantages of a more orderly and democratic style of decision making.

Another aspect of semi-self-government at Achievement Place is the peer manager. In the home there are a number of maintenance activities the boys are responsible for carrying out every day such as straightening the bedrooms, cleaning their bathrooms, bathing, brushing their teeth, and helping with meal preparation. Several procedures for assigning the tasks, evaluating the performance of each individual boy, and administering the reinforcers have been compared. A careful analysis has indicated that several methods are of equal effectiveness in maintaining maintenance behavior. Approximately equal results have been produced by systems involving the teaching-parents assigning the tasks and administering the consequences to each individual youth; the teaching-parents assigning the tasks to each individual youth and then providing consequences on a group basis; and the teaching-parents delegating the responsibility to one of the boys, i.e., a manager for assigning the tasks and consequences to the other boys. After the effectiveness of a particular system has been evaluated, the second most important dimension of a governing system has been the preference of the boys. Six different systems involving managers, individual task assignments, individual consequences, group task assignments, and group consequences have been carefully and systematically evaluated. A system that was effective and also clearly the most preferred by the boys as determined by their votes was an *elected manager* system where the boys elected a manager, each day or each week, who had responsibility for assigning the tasks and consequences to each boy. Also, to our surprise, the boys chose an elected manager system that involved punishment, i.e., the manager could fine as well as give points. When we asked them why they chose this system they made statements that suggested that they preferred a manager who was able to fine boys who didn't work in order to make sure that all the boys worked their "fair share." The boys stated that when a manager had to rely entirely on positive reinforcement he had a problem with some of the boys who had accumulated a large number of points since these boys often would not work for more points. This meant that the other boys, the less wealthy, had to carry out more work. Thus, the boys preferred the elected manager who held the authority to fine those boys who did not work what their peers considered their fair share.

The elected manager system, which involved giving one boy the responsibility to assign tasks and give consequences for the other boys' maintenance behavior, is an effective system and was the preferred system of all the systems that we have compared. This research was important to us in pointing out how powerful a reinforcer the opportunity for choosing their own leaders was for the boys.

The daily behavior report card system, the trial system, and the elected manager system are three examples of behavior modification procedures that are at various stages of development and evaluation at Achievement Place. While a great deal of research remains to be carried out, we feel that the teaching-family model for community treatment of deviant children is ready for dissemination and evaluation on a broader scale.

A training program for teaching-parents is, of course, crucial in the dissemination of the model. We currently have a pilot training program under way to train professional teaching-parents who will be able to establish new homes for delinquent and predelinquent children in their communities. In our opinion, almost any couple that is interested in working intensively with such children and their families should be able to accomplish the objectives of the training program. The training requires about a year. The participants learn various behavior modification procedures such as the management of a token economy. They also have to become proficient in remedial education techniques, food preparation for large families, juvenile law, and community relations. These training objectives are accomplished by a combination of course work and supervised practical experience in the Achievement Place teaching-family setting.

We believe that similar teaching-family programs to train retarded and emotionally disturbed children are feasible. In our expansive moments we envision a teaching-family some day being available in every neighborhood (just as is the neighborhood school) to help train any deviant child and his parents in family and community life skills. It is even possible that teaching-families could be taught to help socialize not only deviant children but many of the deviant adults who are now sent to mental institutions and prisons. Thus, we think that the professional teaching-family concept shows promise as a new model for the treatment of a wide range of human behavior problems in the community.

REFERENCES

Bailey, J. S., Wolf, M. M., & Phillips, E. L. Home-based reinforcement and the modification of pre-delinquents' classroom behavior. *Journal of Applied Behavior Analysis*, 1970, **3**, 223-233.

Cohn, A. *Delinquent boys: The culture of the gang.* Glencoe, Illinois: Free Press, 1955.

Goffman, E. *Asylums: Essays on the social situation of mental patients and other inmates.* Garden City, New York: Anchor, 1961.

Makarenko, A. S. *The road to life.* Moscow: Foreign Language Publ. House, 1953.

Neil, A. S. *Summerhill.* New York: Hart Publ. Co., 1961.

Phillips, E. L. Achievement place: Token reinforcement procedures in a home-style rehabilitation setting for "pre-delinquent" boys. *Journal of Applied Behavior Analysis*, 1968, **1**, 213-223.

Shaw, C., & McKay, H. *Juvenile Delinquency and Urban Areas.* Chicago, Illinois: Univ. of Chicago Press, 1942.

Stuart, R. B. *Trick or treatment.* Champaign, Illinois: Research Press, 1970.

Thrasher, F. *The gang.* Chicago, Illinois: Univ. of Chicago Press, 1939.

Ullmann, L. P., & Krasner, L. Introduction. In L. P. Ullmann and L. Krasner (Eds.) *Case studies in behavior modification.* New York: Holt, 1965. Pp. 1-64.

Wolfensberger, W. The principle of normalization and its implications to psychiatric service. *American Journal of Psychiatry*, 1970, **127**(3), 291-296.

Programming Alternatives to Punishment: The Design of Competence through Consequences[1]

HAROLD L. COHEN

The success of any democratic society is dependent upon the quantity and variety of choice for its citizens. With less opportunity for choice—either because of restricted intellectual, political, or financial avenues—there is less opportunity for a high operational level of democracy. Historically, a society deprived of variety of choice ceases to grow, is confronted with civil disorders, starts to decline, or changes to another form of government.[2]

This paper will cover research in behavior modifications and behavioral engineering programs carried out with adolescents (age 13-18) in a correctional institution for young offenders (Cohen, 1964; Cohen, Filipczak, & Bis, 1967); in a laboratory situation at the Institute for Behavioral Research, Silver Spring, Maryland; and in a public school (Cohen *et al.*, 1970).

The disruptive and antisocial individual is maintained by his environment. The present reinforcement schedules experienced by the student in school,

[1]The writing of this paper and the research described in it were carried out under a grant from the Center for Studies of Crime and Delinquency, National Institute of Mental Health, Grant No. 5 RO1 MH14443-03-CD 1968.
[2]Cohen, Alternatives to Punishment, 1970.

home, and street have been the major support of his delinquent behaviors. A behavior modification program can teach problem children a new repertoire of behavior that will be as rewarding or more rewarding than their old behaviors and thereby less liable to result in antisocial and delinquent acts.

Along with the recorded delinquent behaviors (police and court records), there are behaviors exhibited at school (smoking pot, stealing, damaging school property, aggression toward teachers and students), which in part are being recorded by the school administration. These in-school records of discipline problems help indicate the operant level of what the school communities consider adolescent antisocial behaviors. The correctness of behaviors is, in the main, defined by the social milieu. Each group defines what it considers acceptable behavior. Every environment has a "go" or "no go" message indicating to the behaving individual whether his behavior is appropriate or inappropriate for that group.

When a young man shouts at the top of his voice, jumping up and down, waving his hand wildly, what is the message? Is this a Goldilocks or an Alice in Wonderland problem? Is this behavior exaggerated or is it inappropriate? The only way we can tell is by analyzing more than the topography of the behavior itself. Such a behavior at a college football game is par for the course, but in a public library the behavior is likely to be inappropriate. Also, the final payoff for each may differ. A behavioral examination cannot be complete without an environmental analysis and an objective look at the consequences.

The two programs to be reported in this paper, as well as any research project concerning human behavior, are supported by a complex environment. The environment is made up of the selected subjects, the staff and administration, the physical space controls, and the operating payoff systems (Cohen, 1964). In order to determine what is maintaining a behavior, an examination of the total ecology that surrounds the project must be undertaken and a project designed to measure and deal with the variables that it presupposes as effective. Also, the research methodology must include an objective means of gathering the information needed, in order to determine whether the goals of the research are being carried out. This paper reports the procedures used to carry out these objectives.

LIMITS OF AVERSIVE CONTROLS

Punishment inflicted in a variety of ways has, in the main, kept the antisocial citizen from ravaging the community; however, there have always been those persons who do prey. To cope with them, we have devised various mechanisms of defense: mechanical equipment (fences, walls, closed doors, traps, and alarms) and human and animal equipment (the police, the army, the F.B.I., and the canine corps). A profusion of exclusion and warning devices have been variously "successful."

Unfortunately for the law-abiding and paying citizenry, this form of aversive control works only for those members of society who have acquired alternate routes for achieving success. Those who are unable to gain their needs by socially acceptable methods because of their inadequate environmental and/or intellectual capabilities resort to fulfilling their needs through their limited options: either a bare subsistence or unlawfully usurping the property of the "paying" citizen. For a time, evidence of a dog's presence and the fear of a gun keep the thief away. Eventually, however, having no skills except thievery and still faced with the need and desire to survive at the level of the working group, he returns to raid its accumulated wealth. To counter this behavior, some communities make available a limited subsidy for the needy. Experience indicates that such subsidies are insufficient and must be maintained until death or until the individual develops the necessary skills to "survive on his own." The persistence of youthful offenders, even after "rehabilitation" in our penal institutions and agencies, closely follows patterns which we at the Institute for Behavioral Research (IBR) have observed in our research efforts.

Research over the past ten years (Task Force Report, 1967) has dealt with adolescent youth who are not equipped, academically or vocationally, to fit into our nation's highly evolved socioeconomic structure. We have learned that an adolescent with reading skills at the third grade level who has dropped out of school at the age of 14 years has no real understanding of the larger society around him and has no basic repertoire that will enable him to acquire this understanding. The public school dropout is being maintained in his behaviors by a group of peers who are the same level of educational and cultural deprivation. His opportunity for employment, and therefore his basic source of income, is limited to a rapidly disappearing sector of the labor market—unskilled physical labor. His alternatives for maintaining himself are usually limited to one of three choices: joining one of the Armed Forces (if he can pass the physical and achievement tests), going on relief, or maintaining his subsistence through a variety of antisocial behaviors.

Recent research has refuted the value of lock-up punishment (Phillips, 1968; Glaser, 1964) and increased welfare as methods of dealing with socially unacceptable behavior; and a quick look at the use of police and armed guards provides some additional question as to their effectiveness. IBR's program at the recently disbanded National Training School for Boys in Washington, D.C., 1965-1967 [CASE I (Cohen *et al.*, 1967) and II (Cohen & Filipczak, 1971)] and its present work with delinquent youths who are not institutionalized (Programming Interpersonal Curricula for Adolescents: PICA) under a National Institute of Mental Health grant, 1968-1972 indicate that dropouts will respond favorably to stimulating material and grow academically when a material reward such as money is offered.

REINFORCEMENT PATTERNS

Behavior in any given group of adolescents is the result of a history of successful or unsuccessful performances and their personal payoffs. To presume that criminal behaviors (e.g., car thefts) are the result of similar emotional or financial problems is to presuppose that all youths have the same history. Further, if the case history producing the car thief were standard, then the involvement of police, probation officer, court, fines, sentences, and social rejection should produce the same effect in all the accused. This, in fact, is not the case.

A competent police force, with laws and a judicial system, does work for most Americans (Task Force Report, 1967). Because it has never in the past worked for *all* and still does not now work for all, there are those who feel that the present crime problem lies in society's inability to provide (a) sufficient police coverage; (b) efficient courts, adequate laws, and sufficiently severe punishment; and (c) the reeducation of proper social and moral values. To satisfy these three areas of so-called "fault," we are attempting to legislate means of (a) providing more police and other armed troops; (b) redesigning our courts to increase their efficiency and legislating increased punishments; and (c) reexamining our religious and mental health programs so as to provide in-depth mental and moral therapy.

One of the most difficult tasks is that of eliminating the behavior that has been supported by a series of successes, particularly if the successes happen under varied conditions (Cohen & Filipczak, 1970). In order to change an on-going behavior, society must control the timing and quantity of success. In order to eliminate an old behavior, we must teach the individual alternative responses that can successfully earn him a similar or stronger payoff or behaviors that are competitive and incompatible.

With a certain behavior history, the elimination of specific behaviors without teaching new behaviors is possible (Skinner, 1938). However, the consequences to the individual and the surrounding society may be harmful. Men, in order to raise their families, must work to earn money. We can get people to stop working by refusing to pay their weekly or monthly paycheck, by requiring skills that they do not have, or by racial and class discrimination. In a very short period of time, the majority will have stopped working or looking for work. But there are consequences in stopping their ability to earn the necessary capital for their family support (increase in welfare, crime, riots, and civil war).

Even in a human laboratory situation, the reducing and stopping of an ongoing behavior that has been shaped up with a long and variable history of reinforcement is very difficult. Behaviors most difficult to break are those developed by a variable time interval and variable ratio schedule. Simply, this schedule is called a "slot-machine schedule," that is, sometimes we get paid off after so many tries, two or four or a hundred, and sometimes we get so much reward, two nickels or four or a hundred, for an invested effort. A national dream of the big payoff—hitting the jackpot, getting a raise, becoming the boss, getting elected president, achieving wealth, fame, and success—helps maintain "initiative" and the general productivity of its citizens. Continuation of a democratic society is dependent upon the scattered availability of an eventual "jackpot" in a variety of areas and for a variety of its citizens. It has not been inappropriate that the United States of America has been called "the land of golden opportunity." It was the fulfillment of this schedule for its millions of immigrants—the successful performance payoff for effort expended—that gave the United States its source of strength.

Delinquent youths have been shaped up with such a multiple schedule. Being caught at theft after ten tries, warned, and put on probation; being unsuccessful at one theft, successful at another; sometimes getting a ten-dollar payoff, sometimes hundreds or thousands—a delinquent's theft schedule has in the main followed this slot-machine schedule of reinforcement. Lack of real or consistent success, even over a long period of tries, in no way discourages him from continuing, because the possibility of the big payoff still exists. Even after being caught and incarcerated, a large proportion of the youths return to their delinquent activities following their release from prison.

BEHAVIORAL OPTIONS

We have learned that the major way to change the behavior of a subject shaped by such schedules of reinforcement is by directing the individual to learn new behavioral options under similar schedules. Armed with these new options, which can produce a similar or *larger* payoff, the same youth, under society's threat of punitive action, can take the easier path open to him. Without increasing the aversive control procedures, the threat of punishment can now influence his choice because a meaningful choice now exists.

Simplistically, the reason most people do not steal to gain their reinforcement is that the present aversive control system—religious moral codes with their delayed payoffs; police, law, and courts with their delayed payoffs—directs them to seek safer means of getting their rewards. However, this controllable group does have other repertories to gain success and a large enough payoff. Since most of the youthful offenders we have worked with do not have a variety of rational options available to them (such as employable skills, which have a high payoff), they resort to the one choice that they are equipped to use—unlawful behaviors.

In order to diminish the antisocial behaviors of our delinquent youths, we need to teach them other competitive skills, which in our society produce strong payoffs—money, self-respect, distinction, security, etc. If the payoffs are programmed properly, these new, socially accepted behaviors will gain in strength, making the nonacceptable deviant behaviors incompatible.

At the Institute for Behavioral Research, we have expanded our present resources to further our efforts in research and program development in programs dealing with delinquent youth and those erroneously called predelinquent youth (Cohen, 1970). In order to be effective in this task, we have developed an ongoing operational center, to develop procedures, and the Experimental College of the Institute for Behavioral Research (Catalog, 1970) to train personnel in these procedures. Our major interest is in the young offender and his family. It is for this group that we have been developing an academic, vocational, and interpersonal curriculum that can be taught through a contingency management program within the public school system. In September 1971, we started such programs in 17 public junior high and senior high schools in the Washington area.[3] A description of this curriculum is provided below.

PROGRAMMING INTERPERSONAL CURRICULA FOR ADOLESCENTS (PICA)

Although the PICA Project operates in three parts—the in-house academic/interpersonal program, the public school program, and the PICA parent program—this paper will in general describe the academic/interpersonal section and some of the results.

The basic premise of the PICA Project is that most learning behaviors are related to their consequences, and, by establishing specific learning procedures as well as strict environmental controls, these learning behaviors can be developed, maintained, and extended. There are two aspects to the PICA Project.

1. PICA is a half-day (morning), out-of-school program where teenage, junior high school students study academic matter through special programs. They live at home with their families and attend their respective schools in the afternoons.

2. PICA's learning programs are designed to develop not only academic skills but also appropriate interpersonal behaviors for those students who have had difficulty in this area at school. Examples of these interpersonal behaviors include study habits, interaction with teachers and other school personnel, as well as appropriate interactions with members of the student's family.

Objectives

The PICA project has established a part-time educational program for those adolescents who are viewed by their schools and society as predelinquents or disturbed. The program is designed to investigate experimentally variables that affect academic and interpersonal performance development and to develop learning programs in these two categories. Through the course of this exploration, the project

1. Uses selected self-institutional materials and seminars designed to repair academic deficiencies so that the student will be able to perform the objectives specified by the school as being appropriate for his age level

2. Promotes the learning of study skills so that the student can maintain the academic pace of his school class

3. Attempts to program instructional materials and learning behaviors for interpersonal skills so as to shape performance that does not interfere with academic learning

4. Establishes a system of consequences contingent upon successful

---

[3]The PICA Project, Year II and Behavioral Programs in Learning Activities for Youth (BPLAY).

completion of specified tasks needed to maintain behavior through the learning sessions

5. Develops procedures to promote parental involvement in learning programs structured to assist the parents in dealing with the interpersonal and academic difficulties of their child

6. Develops the program in a manner which promotes its transfer to a normal school program, using school personnel

Academic Program Functions

Approximately 75 self-instructional courses are available for Grades 2-12 in the curriculum areas of English language, reading, and mathematics. Both conventional and modern mathematics techniques are available through most of the mathematics curriculum, assuring continuity with existing programs of local school systems. Each program element is consistent with a major objective of the curriculum guides of the local schools.

Procedures are used that require and permit the student to fulfill behaviorally specified goals for completion of course units within each program in the curriculum. Self-instructional courses and classroom programs are available for the development of academic study skills. Special automated learning programs and devices are used to develop study behavior; present audio, visual, and textual learning materials through programmed and responsive circuitry; and collect student responses covering a range of behavioral dimensions.

Specially designed, automated objective testing apparatus are used both to shape appropriate testing behavior and to assess critical skills such as attention, speed, and accuracy.

Enrichment programs in each of the curriculum areas, which rely on more subjective evaluation, may be taken as part of either the normal activities of the day or as "homework" elements of the program. These are extensions of the self-instructional curriculum materials in which the student is currently proficient.

Each student is permitted to use a private study carrel that is designed to facilitate studying and that can accommodate special automated programming equipment if required.

A reference library has been developed to coordinate with study materials in use. A resource of audiovisual aids (including films, filmstrips, slides, tapes, and models) is readily available for use in and coordination with programs or classes in each curriculum area.

A staff of four full-time and seven part-time educational specialists are involved in the project, including psychologists, educators, designers, teachers, statisticians, and educational aides.

Interpersonal Program Functions

There are two interrelated components of the interpersonal program in PICA: individual interpersonal skills and group interpersonal skills. In the first component, interpersonal skill learning is directed toward increasing each student's ability to interact appropriately with one other student or one staff member at a time. In the group program, each student is trained to deal effectively with groups of other students and teachers.

The individual program is designed to take place within the individualized instructional setting of the academic program. Special sets of behavioral objectives are treated for each student, according to his needs. Individual, student-initiated counseling and training in study skills and self-control procedures are integral components of this program. Successful completion of prerequisites in this area permit the student to advance along a graded series of behavioral levels to positions of greater privilege within the project, both in individual skill programs and in group activities.

Within the group interpersonal skills program, there is a series of four activities in which the students can engage: Design Science, Behavioral Issues, The Contemporary Classroom, and Interpersonal Issues.

In each of these activities, PICA works toward the goal of developing interpersonal skills as prerequisites for succeeding elements in the program. Also, each of the activities was designed from the experience gained during Project Year 1 and has integral objectives set for each topic, ranging through peer relationships, authority relations, family interaction, and self-behavior practices. For each activity, observational skills, language skills, and procedural skills were developed to match explicit criteria for performance standards. Further, each activity approximates the behaviors required of students in differing academic situations: work-study laboratories, traditional classroom lectures, and discussion groups in the "seminar" model.

These facilities, while not austere, represent little cash expenditure for construction, purchase, and maintenance. Project visitors frequently commented that the environment "seemed alive," even when students had left for the day. Typical student graffiti was absent from the facility and only once did a student deface a wall surface (then, only to write her boyfriend's name next to her own on the study booth name place). Accumulations of trash did become a problem in the lounge, but when the staff began charging the students for the clean-up services, such behavior stopped.

MAJOR RESULTS

Twelve junior high school students were referred to PICA because of disruptive in-school behavior, minimal in-school academic performance, and delinquent community activities. These students demonstrated remarkably different behaviors during and following their PICA involvement. Their records with respect to attendance, classroom behavior, and academic performance are summarized in Table 1. Note that this dramatic achievement was obtained with students who had been considered impossible to handle in school——academic failures.

TABLE 1

PICA STUDENTS: SUMMARY OF BEHAVIOR AND ACADEMIC PERFORMANCE

Evaluative factor	PICA students	Basis for comparison
Attendance	82% for PICA year	64% attendance (approximate) for PICA students in previous year 75% attendance (approximate) for normal pupils in three junior high schools from which PICA students were drawn
Average school rating (5 point maximum)	4.2 for all school classes	Comparable figures not available for group
Example: 1 student	2 suspensions during PICA year	79 serious infractions the previous year, resulting in 10 suspensions
Academic performance Failures	3 students received 2 or more failing grades	11 of the 12 students received 2 or more failing grades in previous year
English grades	A-minus average for all PICA students	F average for PICA students in Pre-PICA year
Mathematics grades	A average for all PICA students	D-minus average for PICA students in Pre-PICA year
Mean reading ability	1.6 grade increase in 9 months	0.8 increase per year (approximate) before entering PICA program
Language ability	0.6 grade increase in 9 months	Similar increase in previous years
Mean mathematics, application abilities	1.8 grade increase in 9 months	0.7 grades per year before entering PICA program
I.Q. Assessment (WISC-WAIS) Full-scale score	9.0 point increase in 9 months (sig. 0.0005) (From 20th to 40th percentile)	N.A.
Performance score	10.4 point increase in 9 months (sig. 0.0005) (From 20th to 40th percentile)	N.A.

Follow-up on these students during the current program (two contacts per student) indicates

1. Only two formal juvenile charges placed against students this year, versus seventeen charges the year before program contact.

2. Eight of the twelve students still in school, although all had been considered potential dropouts by school staff.

3. Of the eight students in school, (a) six are maintaining passing grades in most classes, (b) one has unverified grades (out-of-state school), and (c) one is failing four of seven courses.

4. Of the four students not in school, (a) one is seeking accreditation through GED preparation, (b) one is attempting to enroll in a vocational school, and (c) two are full dropouts.

5. Parents of all twelve students report maintenance of good relationships with their children.

THE PICA FACILITY

The physical facility used for PICA Year 2 is in the location employed during Year 1: The IBR Educational Facility, 2401 Linden Lane, Silver Spring, Maryland. Modifications were made to the facility during the summer between Years 1 and 2 to facilitate program changes and to permit working offices for certain key staff. The basic premise of the environmental controls for the Project were extended for Year 2. Facilities were developed that (1) permitted both the observation and shaping of individual study behavior and (2) made possible the modification of in-class behaviors that approximated those required in the students' schools.

No significant modifications were made to the environment during the course of the school year. The following describes the facility as it was used during Project Year 2.

Coordinator's Office

The area of the Coordinator's private office (Fig. 1,A) is also used for staff meetings and for individual conferences with students.

Staff Offices

The staff offices (Fig. 1,B), located at both the front and the rear of the Educational Facility, are used as work areas for the curriculum development specialists, data managers, and other staff. It is also used as a storage area for programs that are not currently in use.

Educational Program-Checking Area

The program-checking station is an area (Fig. 1,C) where the Student Educational Researcher (SER) reports for new assignments, test assignments, work reviews, and specific help that might be needed on his self-instruction work. The area consists of the following sections

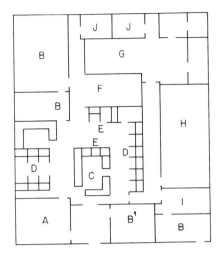

Fig. 1. PICA facility.

1. Two program-checking stations (one for mathematics and one for English), which are used also as storage areas for programs being used in the PICA program.

2. An electronic monitoring system, which is used in the administration of different study programs.

3. Special, industrial-quality time clocks that are calibrated in hundredths of an hour and are used to record the elapsed time for all student activities.

4. Overhead racks where students' work is stored from one session to the next. Located in the same area are other racks in which various supplies used by the program checkers are stored (work sheets, test forms, etc.).

Study Booths

The study booths (Fig. 1,D), which are located on both sides of the program-checking area, are used for all studying and individual work done by the SER. They are constructed of pegboard and Celotex (to help contain as well as to reduce any noise in the working area) and are assigned to each student at the beginning of the semester. Each SER is responsible for keeping his booth clean. Each booth contains a light, a shelf for storage of the SER's books and other personal items, a writing surface, a chair, and the student's name plate. A fine may be levied if the SER does not keep his booth clean.

Testing Booths

There are five testing booths (Fig. 1,E) in the Educational facility. Three of these booths (adjacent to the program-checking station) are used for "paper and pencil" tests. They are separated by a pegboard barrier, which helps prevent communication between students. The other two testing booths contain automatic testing equipment, which may be used in conjunction with the electronic monitoring system located in the program-checking area. These two booths are located across from the "paper and pencil" booths.

Lounge

The student lounge (Fig. 1,F) serves as a place for student rest and diversion (loosely, reinforcement). Students may use the lounge for a short period of time before they begin work in the morning. Following this brief break, and after reporting for work, students are permitted to use the lounge only after having completed a unit of self-instructional work. Further, they must not have received a fine or have been placed on the "time out" bench for misbehavior. They must pay a fee for time spent in the lounge during most of the project year, and their amount of time is limited according to class level achieved in the project. The lounge contains a minimum of amenities: six chairs, a sofa, two tables, soft-drink and candy machines, and a radio. Modern posters and mobiles are the only decorations. Bathrooms (Fig. 1,J).

Student Laboratory

This area (Fig. 1,G) was newly developed for Year 2 to serve as a laboratory for both the Behavioral Issues and Design Science classes. It was outfitted with laboratory tables, demonstration facilities, scientific equipment for conducting operant experimentation with rats, and storage for equipment used in these two classes. The space was used during the last quarter of the project as a general work area for students engaged in scientifically oriented projects under the direction of private tutors.

Classroom

This room (Fig. 1,H) is used for all classroom activities for which objectives demand that they approximate traditional classroom procedures. The Contemporary Problems class, the Interpersonal Issues class, and all student assemblies are held here. The room contains twelve student desks, a teacher's desk, storage space for all class materials, projection screens and both closed-circuit and RF television capability, two television cameras (one static mounted with wide-angle lens for full-room viewing and the other outfitted with a remote controlled pan/tilt mount and zoom lens for detailed viewing), and microphones; there is also a large console for visually displaying bonuses and deductions for in-class behavior (controlled by observers outside the classroom).

Audiovisual Room

This room (Fig. 1,I) contains all audiovisual and control equipment needed to manage the classroom. Two television monitors (one for each camera), controls for the pan/tilt and zoom lens, microphone mixing equipment, and a video recorder comprise the master recording center. Electromechanical counting circuitry and switching controls are also located here to permit direct reinforcement and punishment of classroom behavior based upon the observations made on the TV equipment and recorded on auxiliary forms. Traditional projection and audio recording equipment are housed here for use in class sequences. The room is sound-proofed from the classroom.

Data Management Center

This facility (Fig. 1,B[1]) is designed to house all data management apparatus, equipment, and records. The data manager shares the office with the project assistant. All data records from the student and parent programs of PICA are processed here. Specific program data gathered each project day are listed, filed, processed, and analyzed through a Bell System teletype terminal connected to a time-shared data processing service (Tymshare, Inc.). The resultant information is stored only in this room. Graphic records are made of most data, stored here, and inspected on a project-length (number of days) light table where relations can be made among various data categories. Summary tapes of all processed data are also stored here, to be used at the end of numerous periods (e.g., school grading periods) for the preparation of data-related reports.

PICA DAY IN DETAIL

A typical student's day begins when he boards the PICA bus at his school and is driven to the IBR Educational Facility. As the student enters the facility, he removes his time card from the wall rack, punches the time clock to record the time he entered, and replaces the card. The time clocks are calibrated in hundredths of an hour, so that one-half hour is recorded as 50 hundredths. The student is also responsible for punching out when he leaves the facility, so the time cards provide a permanent record of both the student's attendance and the time spent at PICA.

If the student has a School/PICA Behavior Rating and Homework Scale (discussed later), he places it in the proper slot next to the main time clock. These rating scales are used in cooperation with the SER's school teachers to ensure that the student's behavior in class will be reported to the PICA staff. Included on these forms is a section to be filled in by the student to record homework assignments that will be due the following day. The rating scales are collected, evaluated (students are paid or deductions made accordingly), and a new sheet for the current day's classes is placed in the appropriate place in the rack.

After hanging up their coats and taking care of any personal affairs (bathroom, etc.), the students are permitted to go to the lounge area of the Educational Facility, which contains a soda dispenser and candy machine. The students are allowed to remain in the lounge until they are called over the intercom by a staff member and told it is time to report to the program-checking area.

Upon reporting to the program-checking area, the students are assigned academic work in the form of programmed instruction (PI) or are placed in one of the classes presented during the course of the year. Among these classes are Interpersonal Skills, Design Science, Behavioral Issues, the Contemporary Classroom (study skills), and various special tutorial sessions where one student

Fig. 2. PICA program-checking area

and one staff member meet for two hours per week in a specialized subject (i.e., guitar, basic electricity, office skills, etc.). The above-mentioned classes do not last for the entire morning session of PICA; the student also works on programmed instructional materials.

For each activity in which the students participate, whether it be PI, classroom activities, or staff discussion, a record of where the student is and how long the activity is taking is noted on what the staff refers to as a "pink sheet." This special form is used to record the exact length of time for each activity the student participates in. The forms are completed by the program-checking staff using the time clocks at the program-checking station.

When the student arrives at the checking station, the staff member informs him that he has a Design Science class that day. The program checker records on the student's pink sheet the appropriate symbol (in this case "cl"), initials the sheet, and stamps the time that the student was sent to the classroom. At the completion of this class, the student may go to the lounge, elect to sit on the free bench, or start programmed instructional work. The free bench is the area of the facility (across from the math side of the program-checking station) where the student may sit if he does not feel like working. He is not charged for this activity, but while sitting there he is not allowed to sleep, talk, or exhibit any behavior that might interfere with the other students' work. If he elects to go to the lounge, the time that he enters the lounge is recorded on the pink sheet and the appropriate activity (L) is designated. The student is permitted to take as many lounge breaks as he wants, as long as the total amount of time spent in the lounge does not exceed the established limits of allowable lounge time. Lounge time cannot be accumulated from day to day. When the student returns from

Fig. 3. Student at work in private study booth.

the lounge, the staff member stamps the time on the pink sheet, determines the amount of time spent in the lounge, and notes the charge, if any, to be deducted from the student's earnings.

By referring to the previous day's data, the staff can ascertain how much time the student should spend in each subject. For example, a student who has spent one hour on the previous day working on English, and one hour and 45 minutes in mathematics, must be scheduled for an extra 45 minutes in English to ensure that he spends an equal amount of time in each subject. The student is given an English assignment, which he takes back to his study booth. He works independently until he needs assistance or finishes the assigned material. When this occurs, he reports to the program checker for help or to have his work checked.

All programmed instructional materials at PICA have been evaluated under a uniform system to determine the number of "work units" each program is worth. These work units in turn determine the amount of money the student will receive upon completion of the program at a specific criterion level (90% or 100%). The "work unit" evaluation system will be discussed later. The student is

Fig. 4. Television view of PICA class.

not paid in cash at the time he completes a program; the amount of money he has earned is recorded on the pink sheet. At the end of the PICA day, the data manager pays each student the amount he earned for that day's work. If the student does not complete the program at the specified criterion level, he may still be awarded the work units, but will not be paid until the program (or an alternate form of the program) is completed at 90% or better. In this instance, "money owed" can be held from one day to the next, until the student successfully completes the assigned work.

If at any time during the morning, a staff member feels that a student is behaving in a manner that is interfering with the other students' work, the staff member may place the student on the "forced time-out bench." This bench is actually the same bench used for the free time-out activity. This is a rarely used tactic, but is a control available when the student refuses to behave appropriately.

For illustrative purposes, if a student has been on the forced time-out bench

Fig. 5. PICA student on lounge break.

for more than 0.16 hour, the Project Coordinator calls him into his office to discuss the reason he was placed there. After this conference, the student may be allowed to work or may be sent back to the forced time-out bench. If he continues his work, he will finish the program he started before he was placed on the forced time-out bench.

The student may also, at any time, elect to go to the bathroom or to get a drink of water. This activity is called a study break, and like the other activities, is entered on the pink sheets. At the end of the morning's work, the students are again allowed to go to the lounge without charge. Before the students board the bus that will take them back to school, they are required to pick up their School/Homework Rating Scale and punch their time card. They are then returned to school for the remainder of the day.

THE PICA TESTING BATTERY

The Academic Test Battery

First, standardized tests that related to the proposed academic curriculum were reviewed. It was apparent that the most important test would be in the skill area of reading (which we hoped would include necessary information on vocabulary, speed, and comprehension). Second, it was essential to determine the student's ability to manage mathematical concepts and computation skills in basic arithmetic and mathematics. Both these steps were necessary so that the student could eventually be placed in his appropriate academic level in English and math.

The groups of tests finally selected as the *PICA Academic Testing Battery* were

Gates-MacGinitie Reading Test (Gates)
    Speed and accuracy
    Vocabulary
    Comprehension

Stanford Achievement Test Components (SAT)
    Language components
        Usage
        Punctuation
        Capitalization
        Dictionary skills
        Sentence Sense

    Mathematics components
        Computation
        Concepts
        Applications

Sequential Tests of Educational Progress (STEP)
    Language components
        Listening
        Essay

Individually Prescribed Instruction in Mathematics (IPI)
    Mathematics components
        All pretest sections from entrance test
        Individual skill and level tests, based on student skills

Although these tests served the purposes enumerated above, they fulfilled a further, and more important, program objective. Items on each of these tests could be related specifically to learning objectives stated for the educational program by both the written objectives of PICA and the detailed objectives written for or included in the study materials. Only by this relation of test items and study programs could a program like PICA (or any other well-managed learning program) assess its effectiveness. Such considerations must be made if learning programs are to succeed and be further developed.

These tests were scheduled for administration as an entrance battery and (by using alternate forms of the tests) as interim and post-project assessment. Each student was assigned tests in this series according to his known (or approximate) reading and skill levels. This was accomplished by using one of the test "levels"

TABLE 2
ACADEMIC TEST SCORED AT PROJECT ENTRANCE

Test	Student mean	Range	
		Low	High
Gates			
Speed	5.3	2.0	12.5
Accuracy	5.7	3.5	12.6
Vocabulary	7.8	3.4	12.9
Comprehension	7.9	2.7	12.9
Mean	6.69	2.5	11.9
SAT language			
Mean	6.1	2.0	10.6
SAT mathematics			
Computation	5.4	2.7	9.2
Concepts	6.4	2.3	11.8
Applications	6.0	2.0	10.1

most closely matching current skills (e.g., Primary, Intermediate II, or Advanced levels of the SAT).

The pre-project testing indicated that Year 2 PICA students had a wide range of academic skills and that the instructional program needs would be beyond the range expected before testing. The following table describes the general levels of skill assessed by the most general nationally standardized tests of the battery for Year 2 students at entrance.

Consequently, large-scale program development activities were required during the entire course of Year 2 to ensure that all students would have available to them instructional materials corresponding to their entering and developing skills.

Post-project testing with the same national test instruments indicated that the following gains had been made by PICA students during their nine-month stay in the project:

Obviously, these students' grade-score gains are remarkable in the light of past levels of performance and give evidence that the procedures used within the academic programs to effect this learning must be considered important.

Other Tests and Assessments Used

In addition to the academic battery assembled for PICA, both a standardized intelligence test and a variety of behavioral measures were used in PICA to assess salient behavioral change.

During Year 1, PICA administered, through a psychological testing consultant, a variety of projective tests, which, it was felt, might assist in diagnosing behavior pathology and/or suggesting behavioral remediation. Although no

TABLE 3
MEAN STUDENT GRADE SCORE CHANGE ON
ACADEMIC TESTS FROM ENTRY TO EXIT[a]

Test	Student mean
Gates	
Speed	+1.4
Accuracy	+1.8
Vocabulary	+1.1
Comprehension	+1.0
Mean	+1.55
SAT language	
Mean	+0.6
SAT mathematics	
Computation	+1.4
Concepts	+1.4
Applications	+1.8

[a]September 1969 to June 1970.

rigorous analysis was attempted with the data from these measures, it became clear that the evaluations did not assist in the conduct and development of the Project. First, these assessments tended only to confirm observations made by PICA staff and reports from the students' schools regarding the extent of behavioral deviance. Second, they did not assist in specifying either behavioral objectives for student performance or programs that could be used for shaping appropriate behavior. Consequently, all projective personality instruments were discarded from the PICA entrance battery. The intelligence assessment instruments (WISC and WAIS) were retained for the Year 2 entrance battery. It appeared that these instruments bore some relation to at least the academic components of the program and could be useful in either one of two ways.

1. Either an index of the student's capacity to learn (although this view was doubted) or some indication of his current cultural and academic skills (which seemed more reasonable)
2. (Resulting from the second part of #1), a pre- and post-project assessment of changes in student performance.

Pre- and post-project administrations of these tests (depending on individual student age) were scheduled. Figure 6 represents the results of this testing.

Clearly, even the traditionally accepted view that the full-scale I.Q. on this testing varies only by five points cannot be accepted. These data show a range of I.Q. scores at entrance from 70 to 110, and a range at Project ending of 87 to 121, a mean increase of 9.0 points. This difference demonstrates significance at the 0.0005 level. The verbal subtest of this battery (entrance range, 69-119;

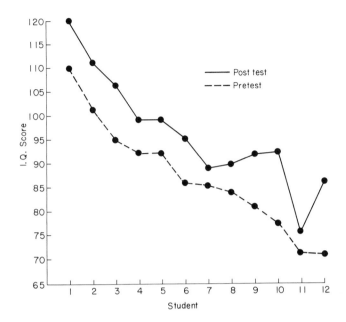

Fig. 6. Pre- and post-project I.Q. test results (WISC-WAIS)—ranked by entrance score.

ending range, 72-123) showed a mean increase of 6.33 points, also significant at a 0.0005 level. The most impressive gains were shown on the performance subtest (entrance range, 60-99; ending range, 72-115) showed a mean increase of 10.4 points, also significant at the 0.0005 level.

REFERENCES

Catalog. Silver Spring, Maryland: Experimental College of the Institute for Behavioral Research, 1970.

Cohen, H. L. Educational therapy. In *Research in psychotherapy*, Vol. 3. American Psychological Association, 1968.

Cohen, H. L. Behavioral architecture. *Architectural Association Journal*, June 1964, pp. 7-12.

Cohen, H. L. Behavioral programs in learning activities for youth (BPLAY). Grant Application to NIMH, May, 1970.

Cohen, H. L. Alternatives to Punishment in Maintaining Law and Order. 138th meeting American Association for the Advancement of Science, Chicago, 1970.

Cohen, H. L., & Filipczak, J. A. A study of contingencies applicable to special education: Case I. In R. Ulrich, T. Stachnik, and J. Mabry (Eds.), *Control of human behavior*, Vol. II. Glenview, Illinois: Foresman, 1970.

Cohen, H. L., & Filipczak, J. A. *A new educational environment*. San Francisco, California: Jossey Bass, 1971.

Cohen, H. L., Filipczak, J. A., & Bis, J. S. *Case I. An initial study of contingencies applicable to special education*. Silver Spring, Maryland: IBR Press, 1967.

Cohen, H. L., Filipczak, J. A., Slavin, J., & Green, D. *The PICA Project—Year II.* Programming interpersonal curricula for adolescents. National Institute of Mental Health, Center for Studies of Crime & Delinquency. Grant No. 1 RO1 MH14443-02 JP, 1970.

Glaser, D. *The effectiveness of a prison and parole system.* Indianapolis, Indiana: Bobbs-Merrill, 1964.

Phillips, E. L. Achievement place: Token reinforcement procedures in a home style rehabilitation setting for "pre-delinquent" boys. *Journal of Applied Behavior Analysis*, 1968, 1, 213-223.

President's Crime Commission. *Task Force Report: Juvenile delinquency & youth crime.* Washington, D.C.; U.S. Government Printing Office, 1967.

Skinner, B. F. *The behavior of organisms.* New York: Appleton, 1938.

Discussion: Methodological Remarks on a Delinquency Prevention and Rehabilitation Program

EMILIO RIBES-INESTA

The paper by Harold Cohen on the PICA project is an excellent illustration of the functioning of a prosthetic motivational system. The design of this system is based exclusively on programming positive consequences for the development of academic, interpersonal, and vocational behaviors.

Several points in this paper invite discussion because of their implications. Some are directly related to technical aspects of the behavioral change assessment within the prosthetic motivational environment; others touch on more fundamental aspects.

DESIGN OF SPECIAL PROSTHETIC ENVIRONMENTS

The PICA project demonstrates how a contingency management system works with subjects classified as predelinquent in developing three kinds of behavior: (1) academic, (2) interpersonal, and (3) vocational. The project, designed as a part-time system, is basically a motivational program focused on establishing behaviors and acquiring knowledge in specific subjects, such as English, arithmetic, etc. Generally speaking, the educational and vocational goals are clearly specified. Sequencing of activities, structuring of contingencies, and

85

the overall design of the environment are favorable for developing study behaviors and generalizing the knowledge acquired. But there is, in my opinion, a serious shortcoming in this behavioral rehabilitation program.

Most of the adolescents attending the PICA project are considered to have become delinquent because of their generalized educational deficits. It would seem, therefore, that the emphasis of the program should be on the design of a highly favorable situation for learning. However, there is, strangely enough, no explicit statement concerning the social deficits in the interpersonal behavior of these subjects. Although there is mention that, through structuring seminars and tasks that promote self-control, the program aims to develop acceptable behaviors, it is evident that this is a poor definition of the behavioral goals, programs, and contingency system through which this development would be fostered.

There is the basic assumption that the development of study and academic behaviors will, by itself, result in the emergence of interpersonal and social behavior, the lack of which has behaviorally defined these subjects as "predelinquent." This is not the place to discuss the legitimacy of this assumption, since we do not have relevant data. However, because of the highly sophisticated techniques used in the prosthetic environment designed by Cohen, it would be worthwhile to take into account this assessment possibility. Is it necessary to specifically program the development of interpersonal behaviors separately from vocational and academic behaviors? What are the topographical and functional dimensions of social behavior that define a subject as predelinquent? Here, again, absence of this possibility of evaluation is still another shortcoming in a prosthetic environment designed to remedy social behavior deficits. How is it possible to appreciate progress in the program, independent of academic and learning achievements? How does one assess the success of a prosthetic social program lacking the objective measures that specify the goals to be pursued? Nevertheless, the hypothesis underlying the PICA project—that the development of appropriate social behaviors is a straight consequence of the successful acquisition of knowledge and a positive learning experience—is fascinating.

BEHAVIORAL MEASURES VERSUS STANDARDIZED MEASURES

Due to the emphasis on the educational aspects of the rehabilitation program, the data presented come from the administration of standardized measurement instruments. These provide a more or less complete picture of the learning achievements of the subjects but lack reference to behavioral measures per se.

Although it is true that standardized measures permit one to compare the subjects with a wider population, they cannot be considered a substitute for the richness of information provided by direct behavioral measures (Risley, Hart, & Reynolds, 1970). Undoubtedly, standardized measures point out gross advancement in the various programs, but it is essential also to have behavioral criteria that allow a finer grain assessment of the effects of the prosthetic system on the acquisition and development of new social and interpersonal repertoires, which are the ultimate goals of the program itself.

This point deserves further elaboration. First, it is evident that standard achievement tests provide measures that show only the amplitude or range of particular verbal repertoires, but they do not yield any data, topographic or functional, concerning behavioral deficits. This is strictly a problem of measurement validity, and since a program designed according to the principles of applied behavior analysis requires the use of measurement instruments that are appropriate to the special techniques, standardized tests fall far short of the mark. Second, is what can be considered one of the most serious weaknesses in current work with behavioral techniques: the failure to specify the relevant dimensions of behavior.

Current practice in behavior modification is characterized, most times, by an indirect and simplistic definition of the response class considered to be the behavior target. Deceptively simplistic criteria for defining behaviors have been adopted, which obscure the fundamental aspects of the response dimension to which the intervention procedure is to be applied. This deficiency is typical in the definition of responses that should have an unequivocal reference to functional aspects of the control exerted by the external environment. An example is the specification of attending behavior as the mere looking at a text, irrespective of its functional relationship with the relevant stimuli. Rodolpho Carbonari, in another chapter, discusses this topic more fully. The problem is even more evident in the area of social behavior, where responses have been defined almost exclusively according to their topographical properties, without taking into account their functional aspects. The exceptions are very few (Lindsley, 1966). Consequently, we must continue to insist on the importance of the design of major behavioral categories in the establishment of prosthetic environments designed to remedy social deficits, even when the design depends exclusively on an optimized learning system based on positive consequences.

GENERALIZATION OF THE EFFECTS OF A PROSTHETIC ENVIRONMENT AND ITS FOLLOW-UP

The basic requirements in any prosthetic program are the procedure for generalizing the achieved changes to the natural environment and the follow-up for an extended period in order to assess their endurance.

Change generalization is attained through the gradual fading out of prosthetic contingencies by means of "transition" stages (Ayllon & Azrin, 1969; Burchard, 1967) and/or redesigning natural contingencies in the external environment. The PICA project describes the structure of a prosthetic environment without mention of any provisions for the generalization of behavioral changes to the social environment outside that setting. The participants in the PICA project attend a neighboring high school for half of the day. It would be interesting to know whether there is also a contingency system in the natural school environment that utilizes teachers, peers, and supervisors who are in close contact with the subjects. Is there any extension of the behavioral program to the familiar environment, to assure the stabilization of the changes in the subject's interpersonal behavior? If so, how are the nonprofessional social agents trained for effective collaboration in the remediation of the behavior deficits of "predelinquent" adolescents?

We ask these questions because we consider the information to be essential for a successful prosthetic program. We have shared in the field of special education the unrewarding experience that the simple structuring of a prosthetic environment without systematic extension to the natural environment turns the specially planned rehabilitation program into a demonstration project. The behavioral change is restricted to the particular environment where contingencies are operating, without any generalization to different situations. The prosthetic environment can be defined as an environment operating basically with arbitrary consequences. If the transition from arbitrary to natural consequences in the social environment is not planned, it is very likely that the behavior change attained under a careful and rigorous programming of the prosthetic environment will be diluted with catastrophic results from any viewpoint. This is precisely one of the most serious technological limitations faced when trying to make the transition between arbitrary and natural consequences (Ferster, 1967) in complex settings.

The second aspect referred to is the follow-up of the behavior changes. Once the goal of a prosthetic program is achieved, and the assumption is made that the changes have generalized to the natural environment, it is still necessary—not only necessary, but essential—to evaluate the endurance and stability of a change. In order to carry out a *useful* and relevant follow-up, we must accurately define the most important behavior categories and the circumstances under which they must be emitted. Deficiencies in the follow-up techniques presently at our disposal reveal two aspects: (1) lack of specification of criterion behavior and (2) lack of controls. Both omissions, in the long term, impede our efforts to evaluate the promoted behavior changes. If we do not pay more attention to these two major concerns in the evaluation of the final products of our prosthetic programs, we will be lulling ourselves into a sense of false security about the objectivity and efficiency of our applied technology.

DETERMINANTS OF DELINQUENT BEHAVIOR

As Cohen has pointed out, in agreement with some other writers (Burgess & Akers, 1966), delinquent behaviors are determined by two factors in the social environment. The first one is the intermittent reinforcement that maintains delinquent behavior. Usually, delinquents are not caught every time they actually commit an offense, so the proportion of reinforcement versus nonreinforcement of the delinquent behavior is very high. This seems the most acceptable explanation for the prolonged endurance of the antisocial behavior. The second factor is that there are delayed aversive consequences for the delinquent behavior, due, as a rule, to a lag in the legal process. This aversive contingency system, which, as history has proven, is notably ineffectual, provokes avoidance behaviors by the delinquent that remove him even more from the social gratifications (reinforcements) available from the community to those who adhere to the group rules. This sets up the typical vicious circle. The delinquent develops an active avoidance of the aversive consequences imposed by society on those behaviors that give him the highest pay-off and reinforcement. On the other hand, he becomes unable to receive more appropriate forms of social reinforcement, since his peer group prescribes specific contingencies in this regard. Therefore, the delinquent creates his own community. New reinforcement rules, different behavioral dimensions, and new interaction patterns are set up that eliminate almost any possibility of incorporating the delinquent individual to society (Patterson & Reid, 1970).

This multiple determination of delinquent behavior points out the need to go beyond traditional solutions and find new or different approaches to the problem. From a behavioral viewpoint, the delinquent shows a deficit or absence of appropriate social behaviors that would enable him to obtain reinforcement from society and that might encourage him to abandon prohibited sources of gratification (his own delinquent behavior). It is obvious, then, that the source itself of delinquent behavior lies in the inability of society to provide to all its members the appropriate contingencies to promote the development of the kinds of repertoires that would be reinforced. Therefore, the attack on this problem must be directed toward the environment that has generated the delinquent behavior.

PROSTHETIC ENVIRONMENTS VERSUS DIRECT INTERVENTION ON SOCIAL ENVIRONMENT

In considering the overall strategy to the problem of delinquent behavior, two solutions stand out. One, with limited scope, is through the design of prosthetic environments. Here, subjects showing delinquent behavior are retrained under optimal conditions in a specially planned environment. The number of individuals that can be accommodated in this way is far too small, and the expense is much too prohibitive over a long period. Nevertheless, it is an approach that can be adapted to existing penal and reformatory institutions. The objective would be to re-program their functioning by transforming traditional lock-up institutions into rehabilitation centers, carefully designed according to behavioral criteria and with personnel trained in the use of contingency management. As they are now run, penitentiaries and reformatories are almost perfectly programmed centers for training in criminal behavior. Their functional restructuring, besides fostering the rehabilitation of inmates, would help to eradicate one of the major sources of maintenance of delinquent behavior.

Another more desirable way of coping with the problem of delinquency is through *prevention*. Since we have attributed the origins of delinquent behavior to the inadequate organization of society, we are obliged to look for a solution, and as I see it, this solution calls for a radical change or restructuring of the whole social environment. Unfortunately, agencies exerting the social controls are not precisely the entities most receptive to this kind of change. On the contrary, these social agencies themselves become social structures that tend to maintain and perpetuate the *status quo*. Although complete change is a desirable first step, we must sensibly put aside revolution as a technique for behavior change since this requires not only certain technical capacities but also the conjunction of many other factors foreign to the psychologist as a behavioral engineer.

Although we cannot produce a radical transformation in the structure of the contingencies system that favors the emergency and maintenance of delinquent behavior, we are able to approach this change at least at a micromolar level. A preventative program would consist of (1) locating urban, suburban, and rural areas in which present conditions foster delinquent behaviors, (2) behaviorally assessing the design of this population nucleus and the positive ways of restructuring the environment, and (3) intervening directly to modify the structural and functional aspects of the environment, aiming to develop a local contingency system adequate for developing socially acceptable behaviors.

We have indicated, then, that a program for suppressing delinquent behavior can be put into effect in at least two ways: one, in the establishment of prosthetic environments that will attempt to rehabilitate those already committed and the other, in the redesigning of communities or social groups characterized by a high incidence of delinquent behaviors. The latter alternative, which, as we indicated earlier, presupposes direct intervention on the natural social environment and constitutes an almost totally unexplored field that requires new techniques of planning and evaluation.

DEMONSTRATION VERSUS SERVICE PROJECTS

The previous analysis leads us to consider the difficulties and problems encountered in implementing an integral program for the reduction of incidence of delinquent behavior in Latin America, with its high rate of delinquency, limited financial resources, deficient penitentiary system, and lack of trained technical personnel to cope with the rehabilitation of the delinquent.

The arrangement of a prosthetic environment requires the availability of at least three elements: (1) financial resources that allow for the design of projects similar to PICA, (2) enough behavioral technicians and behaviorally trained paraprofessionals to handle the responsibilities of a project of this nature, and (3) adequate installations that allow for a gradual transition from highly controlled prosthetic environments to intermediate institutions and, finally, to the social environment in a given community.

It is evident that such a program is not feasible at this time, if for no other reasons than those mentioned above. These limitations would reduce the strength of the project to just a few rehabilitation centers, which, operating in the general context provided by the social group, would, as I said earlier, merely be simple demonstration projects and not the service projects so badly needed.

The most feasible alternative is to try to develop an intervention program in the community itself, using existing institutional facilities (carefully redesigned) as rehabilitation and temporary detention centers for those delinquents whose behavior might be physically dangerous to society. The direct intervention on some particular nucleus of the community (accepting the impossibility of modifying the overall social organization) provides a number of advantages worthy of consideration.

The first, and perhaps the most important, is an attack on the root of the problem—modification of those aspects of the social environment that foster delinquent behaviors. The direct alteration of those conditions represents a preventative action with far-reaching consequences in terms of the number of individuals affected, compared to the establishment of prosthetic systems confined to purely *individual* rehabilitation functions. The programming and designing of a community organization constitute a rehabilitation intervention of the *social environment,* to the extent that this is feasible.

Second, rather than a "clinical" work, this intervention represents a behavioral engineering or architectural task. This task comprises the urban design of the habitat system, recreation areas, normative control systems, labor sources—all of which professionals provide under *normal* conditions. It does not require extraordinary resources in personnel or facilities, since the intervention is based on the rational use of available or minimal resources (they may need to be created in extremely poor areas) and the design of social contingency systems, programmed and managed by the social agencies of the community itself.

Third, the system allows for a continuous design refinement that generalizes itself to different situations. The social group members are trained to think and evaluate their actions, not only in relation to delinquent behaviors, but also to a varied range of social behaviors.

Such an approach, although assuming the development of a sophisticated technology for carrying out this program, does not encounter limitations in the group members or even in the individuals classified as delinquent. All of them operate under the contingencies imposed on their behavior by the social structure. The ultimate possibilities of a far-reaching action such as the one sketched here depend on how reinforcing this change is to the social control agencies. It not only suggests a stimulating project for the modification of the social environment and the prevention of delinquent behavior but also stresses the importance of the assessment of the reinforcers for those who control the social agencies that structure and regulate the general conduct of the community.

REFERENCES

Ayllon, T., & Azrin, N. H. *The token economy: A motivational and rehabilitation system.* New York: Appleton, 1969.

Burchard, J. D. Systematic socialization: A programmed environment for the habilitation of antisocial retardates. *Psychological Record*, 1967, 17, 461-476.

Burgess, R. L., & Akers, R. L. A differential association-reinforcement theory of criminal behavior. *Social Problems*, 1966, 14, (2), 128-147.

Ferster, C. B. Arbitrary and natural reinforcement. *Psychological Record,* 1967, **17,** 341-347.
Lindsley, O. R. Experimental analysis of cooperation and competition. In T. Verhave (Ed.), *The experimental analysis of behavior.* New York: Appleton, 1966.
Patterson, G. R., & Reid, J. B. Reciprocity and coercion: Two facets of social systems. In C. Neuringer and J. L. Michael (Eds.), *Behavior modification in clinical psychology.* New York: Appleton, 1970.
Risley, T., Reynolds, N., & Hart, B. The disadvantaged: Behavior modification with disadvantaged preschool children. In R. H. Bradfield (Ed.), *Behavior modification: The human effort.* San Rafael, California: Dimension Publ., 1970.

The Entrée of the Paraprofessional in the Classroom

K. DANIEL O'LEARY

In the face of severe criticisms of educational programs, politicians and school administrators in many countries are actively campaigning for more school personnel. In contrast, the taxpayer decries the already soaring educational costs and votes down school budgets requesting more teachers. Nonetheless, he demands more service than he is currently receiving. One obvious method of dealing with the lack of professional personnel is to hire paraprofessionals or to request that volunteer paraprofessionals be brought into the school. Schools that lack mechanical reinforcement dispensers, that lack teaching machines, and that lack teachers who can attend frequently to a child with special difficulties in a classroom of 30 children, may find the paraprofessional a ready solution to many problems in the classroom. In fact, in Mexico, where classes are often larger than 50 and where research money is scarce, the paraprofessional offers many special advantages. Viewed by a taxpayer, the paraprofessional would appear to be an economical dream. Viewed by a parent, however, the paraprofessional may be seen as a poor man's teacher. In the teacher's union's eyes, the paraprofessional has been seen as a threat to both status and job security. In short, the paraprofessional is arriving as a mixed blessing, and his presence may be viewed positively or negatively depending upon one's vantage point. It is my opinion, however, that his advantages far outweigh his disadvantages, and I will present both a rational and an empirical justification of that opinion.

Before discussing the role of the paraprofessional and research related to his utilization, let me first define what I mean by a paraprofessional. A paraprofessional is someone who works with or along side a person who has a professional degree, license, or certification. The paraprofessional may be a physician's aide, a psychological technician, a teacher aide, or a tutor. At the moment, I am limiting my use of the term paraprofessional to adults who are assisting a professional. At a later point, I will discuss the use of peers who can serve many of the same functions as paraprofessionals but who present a number of unique advantages and disadvantages.

All too frequently, when new treatment programs or new manpower utilization procedures are developed, public acceptance of such programs and procedures precedes research evaluation. This is certainly the case with paraprofessionals. For a number of reasons, schools are not willing to wait for such evaluations, or they feel that it is not needed. Particularly in poverty areas where manpower problems prevail, many schools already employ paraprofessionals. Let us look at some of the factors that make the role of the paraprofessional seem a certainty in schools in the future, i.e., let us look at some of the social-political factors related to the adoption of the parapro-fessional that are largely independent of the research evaluation to date.

Despite the disadvantages of the paraprofessional and the opposition to his presence in the classroom, a number of the following trends in education appear to be thrusts that will assure the paraprofessional an important place in all classrooms of the year 2000 or even earlier.

1. Though teacher's unions initially feared the presence of teacher aides, unions are now representing aides and requesting their presence more frequently in the classroom. The teacher's unions are involved in lobbying and direct legislative efforts to secure more and more aid from paraprofessionals. Furthermore, the teacher aides, though presently underpaid, are now repre-sented in some areas by the United Federation of Teachers, a subsidiary of the AFL-CIO, and one does not need much foresight to realize that the teacher aides will soon request the presence of more aides in their midst. That is, paraprofessionals will be asking for more paraprofessionals.

2. The utilization and licensing of physician's assistants who can perform routine physical examinations and execute certain diagnostic tests provides a strong model for *other* paraprofessionals. The training of medical assistants has grown astronomically in the past few years, and since the medical profession exerts such a strong influence on other professional groups, there is ample reason to believe that their role will be an important one. That is, as the medical paraprofessional is able to perform jobs requiring technical skill but not a medical degree and—equally important—as he is well compensated for such skills, other paraprofessional groups will follow the lead set by the physician's assistants concerning career ladders, salary scales, and job conditions.

3. The emphasis on youth sparked by Head Start and Follow-Through and more recently by the President's Council on Youth will also make the utilization of paraprofessionals very likely. Francine Sobey (1970) who reviewed 185 NIMH sponsored projects involving paraprofessionals recommended that there should be greater emphasis on the early periods of life and that a focus must be placed on problem prevention at an early age via a total community approach. While the title of this paper refers to the classroom, we must reemphasize that, if we are to have long-range and general impact educationally, an educational program must often do more than focus on the classroom. Dr. Wahler (1969) has demonstrated that changes in classroom behavior do not always imply changes in similar behaviors at home. Furthermore, the results of national evaluations of Head Start programs in the United States have found that without follow-through, appropriate behaviors will soon disappear (extinguish). Consequently, in a number of educational programs, the peers and parents must be taught to reinforce a child's educational efforts as well as his social behavior at an *early* age, and the paraprofessional—as I will document later—is in a good position to see that reinforcement of such behavior occurs.

4. As more economical methods of teaching are developed by industry and private research organizations, school systems may be pressured to adopt similar procedures. Private industry has already contracted to teach reading in a number of school systems across the country, and we can be assured that industrialists will not hire people with advanced degrees if they can get the same job done by people with lesser degrees. That is, why should they pay a certified person $8000 when they can pay a paraprofessional $3000 to do almost the same teaching job? In short, the use of the paraprofessional seems inevitable by industrial firms. If these industrial firms are successful in reaching their goals, and if they can do so less expensively than the public schools, the taxpayers who have been vetoing school budgets will eventually pressure the school system to hire paraprofessionals.

5. Another factor that will probably increase the need for paraprofessionals is the reemerging emphasis on a free or informal classroom. In his new book, *Crisis in the Classroom*, Silberman (1970) has portrayed present school systems in extremely bleak terms. He dubs the standard public school method as the "chalk and talk" routine in which children sit in rows of desks and are asked to keep their hands folded. He states that the most important characteristic schools share is a preoccupation with order and control. Whereas Silberman rejects John Holt's (1964) notion that children should simply be turned loose to do their own thing, he strongly advocates an adoption of the informal classroom now practiced by many elementary schools in England. Nyquist, State Commissioner of Education in New York, has already advocated the adoption of an informal approach to schooling as an antidote to what is described as the "joyless schools of today" (Nyquist, 1970). Such joyless schools are characterized by a teacher who starts and directs all instructional activities and in which each child is expected to do the same thing at the same time. The free school is characterized by a workshop-like atmosphere in which "interest areas" take the place of rows of desks and chairs. Silberman describes the class as follows.

Not even the most informal American kindergartens have the incredible richness and variety of materials found in the average informal English infant or junior school classroom. The reading corner, for example, typically is an inviting place, with a rug or piece of old carpet on which children may sprawl, a couple of easy chairs or perhaps a cot or old couch for additional comfort, and a large and tempting display of books at child's height. The arithmetic (or "maths," as the English call it) area most likely will have several tables pushed together to form a large working space. On the tables, in addition to a variety of math texts and workbooks, will be a box containing rulers, measuring tapes and sticks, yardsticks, string, and the like. . . . There is no need to have a seat and desk for each child: the teacher seldom instructs the class as a whole, and when she does, the children simply gather around her, pulling up chairs or sitting on the floor. . . . At any one moment, some children may be hammering and sawing at a workbench, some may be playing musical instruments or painting, others may be reading aloud to the teacher or to a friend, still others may be curled up on a cot or piece of carpet, reading in solitary absorption, oblivious to the sounds around them [221-223].

The free or informal school approach has been implemented by teachers who have at least 30 children. However, except for anecdotal reports there is little or no evidence documenting the superiority of the free classroom over the more structured classroom (Silberman, 1970). It is the author's opinion that the informal classroom will succeed only if the children receive direction and guidance—and here the paraprofessional may again be of help. Skinner (1969) noted in discussing the "free school," that simply to abandon punishment and allow students to do as they please is to abandon the goals of education. He adds that the free school dream has failed because such a school does not give children a reason for studying and learning. Skinner, as is generally known, believes that such "reasons" about why men behave are to be found in the consequences of their behavior—i.e., what they get out of behaving. It should be emphasized, however, that many of the principles of reinforcement are not at all incompatible with many of the procedural aspects of an informal school system. In fact, a wedding of reinforcement principles and some aspects of the informal school system such as working at one's own rate and frequently working on subject matter of one's choice could do much to dispel the association of behavioral principles with an autocratically run school. Reinforcing a child for remaining in his seat and being quiet is very important to teachers in most schools as they are currently run, and behavioral psychologists have well demonstrated that teachers can obtain quiet by following reinforcement principles (O'Leary & O'Leary, 1972). However, if a paraprofessional were in every classroom, the need for control and quiet would be less of an issue to every teacher, and some of the freedom of the free school could be allowed without any sacrifice of the teacher's academic goals. Though the free school system has been buttressed with arguments from Rousseau, Piaget, Dewey, and more currently from Neil, it is unlikely that, in an age of cost accountability, parents will ever allow the freedom described by Neil. That is, parents will demand to know rather specific progress goals at various steps of the child's development. They will want to know on what level the child reads, what portion of children in such schools go to college, etc. Such pressure on the one hand for accountability and on the other for an end to the repressive and formal aspects of many of todays schools may result in a combination of some of the informality of the free school and the specificity and direction advocated by behavioral psychologists.

6. Probably one of the most important factors that will influence the use of adult and child paraprofessionals as teachers is the conceptualization of the teaching process in a hierarchical fashion. Ulrich and his associates (Ulrich, Louisell, & Wolfe, 1972, in press) have titled such a view "pyramidal instruction" where advanced graduate students teach less advanced graduate students, graduate students teach upper level undergraduate courses, advanced undergraduates teach introductory courses, etc. As Ulrich and others have mentioned, extension of this notion of pyramidal or hierarchical instruction can easily be envisioned for the public schools. There might be a master teacher with several adult paraprofessionals and perhaps several student aides for classes in both elementary and high schools. One of the most important aspects of pyramidal instruction is the view that children can teach other children. The harnessing of "child power" in the schools is long overdue since the benefits both to the child-teacher and to the child who is being taught are unestimable. As will be exemplified later, grade-school children have been taught behavioral principles and have implemented them successfully in treatment programs.

In summary, the adult paraprofessional may be a solution to a number of the current crises in education, and the trends in present-day education will presumably assure the paraprofessional of a strong role in the educational systems of the future. In fact, paraprofessionals are so potentially important that one might ask why they have not been used more extensively in the school systems before. Indeed, if they are useful and inexpensive one wonders why their adoption is opposed in many quarters. One of the reasons I have encountered repeatedly is that principals and superintendents fear their presence. Even where women's organizations in a community have *volunteered* their help in individual tutoring or in classrooms, superintendents have been reluctant to allow them entrée into the schools. School officials fear that parents and community members will begin to exert undue control in the schools. In a very real sense, some of their fears are well founded, for as community members learn more about schools they also demand a greater voice in their operation. The fights over community control of schools in the past few years attest well to this fact. The paraprofessional is taught certain skills he can use in a classroom or in tutorial sessions, but he may well envision new roles for himself that were not in his job description.

The paraprofessional has sought and obtained entrée in the poverty areas of our country probably more often than in other socioeconomic sectors. There the paraprofessional sees that Johnny's failure to read is not simply due to the lack of an adequate technology for teaching reading. In many cases Johnny's failure to read may be due to the fact that he is hungry, that he can't see properly, that he is a victim of lead poisoning, or that he cannot sleep because the heat in his building is not on. Such stresses lead paraprofessionals—even more strongly than teachers—to become active politically and occasionally even militantly active. Furthermore, as the paraprofessional sees that his performance equals that of the professional, he gains the job security and confidence to demand more pay—as was evidenced in New York City's Mobilization for Youth Project. In Topeka, Kansas, 60 psychiatric aides assumed control of eight hospital wards and demonstrated how they should be run (Sobey, 1970). This activism is greatly feared by some school officials. While such fears are well founded, there is little that can be done to stem the rising tide of paraprofessionals with their political prowess. Even if the tide could be changed, I think it would be a grave disservice to our youth. In many ways we are not giving all children an equal right as they enter the educational arena, and the right of high quality education for all children seems long overdue.

As mentioned by Sobey in her book *The Nonprofessional Revolution in Mental Health*, the paraprofessional is definitely creating new roles for himself. In fact, some people have derided the industrial model of teaching specific skills to the paraprofessional because of the restricted outlook such training might create. Whereas I can empathize with the goal of such a notion, if paraprofessionals are not trained to perform specific educational tasks in the schools, their roles will be severely undermined. In fact, teachers would probably be well advised to assign paraprofessionals tasks which are well delineated. Giving them such tasks does not mean that they cannot teach—they can! It does mean, however, that the paraprofessional should be given teaching assignments where it is likely that he can succeed. Throwing a paraprofessional into an unstructured situation with ill-defined goals and ill-defined methods of reaching those goals will only lead to greater dissatisfaction and greater militancy concerning the school crises. Furthermore, teaching a paraprofessional specific instructional skills is not at all incompatible with the possibility of his creating new roles for himself as a paraprofessional, which will be beneficial to all concerned. Education is too long ill ridden with ambiguous jobs and ambiguous methods of filling those jobs for us not to emphasize some specific task training.

EVALUATION

We have discussed a number of trends that I feel will assure the paraprofessional of a role in the classroom. However, these factors are not derived from research evidence. They are primarily political or economical. Since the ultimate status of paraprofessionals depends (or should depend) on the evaluation of their contribution to education, let us turn to an assessment of some of the uses of the paraprofessionals to date—particularly, though not exclusively—as evidenced by those researchers who have employed a behavioral conceptualization.

Ryback and Staats (1970) trained parents to use a token reinforcement procedure to teach reading to their children. The failure to read is displayed by a large number of children, but heretofore there has been little evidence that this particular skill could be taught effectively by a parent. Four children with reading problems, who ranged in age from 8½ to 13, were selected for this study. The mothers of these children had completed high school; they had an estimated average I.Q. of 102, and an average reading score on the WRAT of 12th grade.

Because the specification of training procedures is critical in paraprofessional programs and because the Staats method of tutoring served as a prototype for other studies, which I will describe, the Ryback and Staats procedure is presented in some detail. The training materials were based on the Science Research Associates (S.R.A.) Reading Laboratory Books and included stories that have a graded introduction of new words in each lesson. Each new word in a story was presented to the child on a 5" X 8" card before he read the story.

> Each new word is presented as a stimulus; if the child cannot read the word, he is prompted. The children learn to read each word to a criterion of one correct unprompted reading, each word being deleted from the series as criterion is reached. Following this, the paragraphs of the story are read by the child. The child is prompted on any words he cannot read, and the paragraph is re-read, if necessary until it is done perfectly [p. 112.]

Then follows silent reading and S.R.A. questions of comprehension. Whenever a question was missed, the child reread the relevant paragraph in the story and responded to the question again. In sum, each lesson consisted of

1. Individual word learning
2. Oral paragraph reading
3. Silent reading
4. Comprehension questions

In addition, a vocabulary review was presented following every 20 lessons to test the child's retention. The token reinforcer system included tokens or plastic chips of three different colors representing $\frac{1}{10}$ of a cent, $\frac{1}{5}$ of a cent, and $\frac{1}{2}$ of a cent. Daily recording of the child's progress was presented to him with approval if appropriate. Disapproval, nagging, and urging to do well were discouraged. In exchange for the tokens, the child could buy inexpensive items such as candy bars or more expensive items if he saved for longer periods of time. The mean cost of reinforcers per child over a 5- to 7-month period was $18.34. It is important to note that different kinds of reading were selectively reinforced so that the child was more heavily reinforced for reading a word correctly on his first attempt than if it were his second attempt—and as might be guessed he was highly reinforced for answering comprehension questions correctly.

Parents were trained for four hours—initially in a didactic manner and later in a direct supervisory manner when the parent was with the child. Special emphasis was placed on behavior recording, and there was a checklist used to evaluate the parents' behavior, e.g., to evaluate the delivery of tokens, the filling out of the token graph, the manner of materials presentation, etc.

The pre- and posttest materials consisted of words randomly selected from the 4200 words used in the reading materials. Two alternate forms of the test were developed and matched for difficulty according to the Thorndike-Lorge word count. The pretest reading mean was 46, and the posttest mean was 86, indicating that the children had improved significantly (*t*-test $p < 0.01$). An additional pre- and postevaluation was made via the Spache Diagnostic Reading Scales. On *all* three subtests, word recognition, instructional level, and a comprehension level test, there was a significant increase in achievement. These increases are particularly significant since they indicated that the training was not limited to the particular materials involved. Furthermore, as a partial control condition, two siblings of two of the four experimental Ss were given pre- and postreading assessments when the experimental Ss received such testing. Neither of the siblings advanced significantly.

A number of professionals would view the tutoring of a child with social and emotional problems rather dimly, because they would fear that the interaction between the parent and the child would prevent any gains from tutoring. It is interesting to note that in this study by Staats and Ryback, the children's problems included mental retardation, emotional disturbance, and cerebral dysfunction. It should be emphasized, however, that the parent-child interaction was supervised directly, and one mother had to be discouraged from various forms of social censure (tone of voice and annoyance). In summary, a relatively short parent training period of 4 hours and some ongoing supervision in the child's home was enough to significantly increase the reading skills of children with a variety of social and academic problems.

Becker and his associates studied the relationship between teacher behavior and a child's appropriate behavior in a classroom (Becker, Madsen, Arnold, & Thomas, 1967). They assessed the use of contingent teacher attention by observing the frequency of various disruptive behaviors during a baseline period. Following this baseline period, the teacher was given instructions to make the rules explicit for her class by reviewing them twice during the morning and afternoon sessions. In addition, the teacher was asked to reinforce or attend to behaviors such as paying attention and staying in one's seat and to ignore as much of the child's disruptive behavior as possible. Becker and his associates (Becker et al., 1967) found that the rules and praising appropriate behavior and ignoring disruptive behavior were quite successful in increasing on-task classroom behavior in seven out of ten children. With one child, Dan, a fourth grader functioning at the second grade reading level, ignoring disruptive behavior and praising appropriate behavior resulted in only small improvement in on-task behavior. However, on-task behavior improved dramatically with the addition of a half-hour of remedial reading each day by a paraprofessional.

In order to examine more precisely the effects of tutoring on a child's level of disruptive behavior, a further study concerning teacher attention and tutoring was implemented (Thomas, Nielson, Becker, & Kuypers, 1968). In the present case, another child's on-task behavior was increased by the use of a teacher's praising appropriate behavior and ignoring disruptive behavior, but it seemed to be accelerated markedly by the use of tutoring following the Staats procedures for remedial reading (Staats & Butterfield, 1965). The remedial tutoring was conducted by a junior psychology major. In addition to earning points (marks on a card) exchangeable for back-up reinforcers (prizes) in the tutoring session, the child could earn points for completing workbook assignments in class. The child's score on the reading portion of the Wide Range Achievement Test before tutoring was 1.4. After 30 tutoring sessions lasting 21 hours, extending over 6 weeks, and costing $5.50 in prizes, his score improved to 2.0. His scores on the Illinois Test of Psycholinguistic abilities increased from 6 years 4 months to 6 years 10 months. Gains of a year or more occurred on four subjects.

Ross and Nelson in our Child Psychological Clinic at Stony Brook (personal communication, December, 1970) have successfully used college students as tutors for twelve elementary school children. The Sullivan Programmed Reading Series was the text for their tutoring program. Children received points for correct responses in the reading series, and the points were exchangeable for small prizes at the end of the tutoring sessions. The children were tutored three times per week for fifteen weeks, and the tutors received eight seminars during the sixteen weeks as well as ongoing supervision. The seminars consisted of readings in behavioral analysis and its application to reading, e.g., discussion of reading as an operant, token reinforcement procedures, and programmed instruction. The children who were tutored were compared with matched controls who did not receive tutoring. The tutored children made significantly greater gain in reading than the controls on three of the five standard reading measures.

A Homework Helper Program in New York City where high school boys and girls tutored elementary students provides evidence not only about the success of the person being tutored but also about changes in the tutors' behavior (Cloward, 1967). Whereas the authors of this program did not espouse a behavioral model, their measurement of the effects of a tutoring program on the reading achievement of both the tutor and the tutored child is unique and it is one of the most interesting studies to date. There were 356 experimental subjects who received tutoring by 240 high school students for five months, and 157 control subjects who did not receive tutoring. Most of the tutors were in tenth grade and the children receiving tutoring were in fourth or fifth grade. As I mentioned before, the program did not espouse a behavioral approach to tutoring and in contrast to other work by Staats in which children made significant gains with 35-65 hours of tutoring, reading improvement was found here only when tutorial aid was given as many as 4 hours a week for 26 weeks (104 hours). Such results would seem to argue strongly for a well-outlined reinforcement "theory" approach for the tutors, which was not provided by Cloward. Much more important than the results of the children being tutored, however, were the gains made by the tutors. During the five-month period, the tutors made significant gains in reading skill. In fact, the tutors showed a mean growth of 3.4 years, whereas the controls gained only 1.7 years. As Cloward notes, employing potential high school dropouts as reading tutors might be much more successful in eliminating reading deficiencies than many of the existing pre-employment programs for students with large academic deficiencies.

In an exciting, innovative project, Tharp and Wetzel (1969) trained para-professionals whom they called "Behavior Analysts" to institute behavior change programs in a child's natural environment. The behavior analysts were selected specifically because they lacked training in the mental health professions; they were selected for "intelligence, energy, flexibility, and personal attractiveness." They included a housewife, a cocktail waitress, a former carpenter, a football player, etc., with an average age of approximately 20 years. Their *sole* training was a three-week seminar involving the use of behavioral concepts (e.g., materials taken from Bijou & Baer, 1961; Bandura & Walters, 1963; Ullmann & Krasner, 1965), research applications, and "on the job" training by a supervising psychologist. The children with whom they worked were referred by the public school and displayed a wide variety of problems. There were both boys and girls in the sample and they ranged from 6 to 16 years in age. Relevant to the topic here, viz., the classroom, a number of children were chosen because of misbehavior at school and underachievement. All children had I.Q.'s greater than or equal to 90. The behavior analyst (B.A.), upon acceptance of a referral, visited the school himself and began the assessment phase—interviewing teachers and school personnel, making classroom contacts, and recording the occurrence of problem behaviors. Although the supervising psychologist was accessible to the B.A. during the assessment phase, there was minimal supervision during this time. Following the assessment, the B.A. met with his supervisor and planned an intervention program that the B.A. presented to the school and/or parents, i.e., to those people who would mediate the treatment. During treatment, phone calls and visits by the B.A. were frequent (often daily) and central to the program. The B.A. held no office hours but rather worked in the schools per se. The data collected by the mediator (i.e., teacher or parent) indicated that of the 36 cases involving poor academic work, 34 improved. Behaviors included in the "academic work" category included completion of assignments in class and homework. Of the 20 cases involving disruptive behavior (throwing objects and talking out of turn) 16 showed improvement. Of the 7 cases evidencing tardiness, 4 showed improvement. Grade changes did not occur. While the data from this project are subject to mediator biases and absence of controls (either single subject or group controls), the Tharp and Wetzel program is an exciting attempt to utilize paraprofessional manpower.

Probably the largest projects to involve paraprofessionals where a behavioral model is employed are the Head Start Follow-Through programs of Englemann-Becker based at the University of Oregon and the Bushell program based at the University of Kansas. Because of greater personal familiarity with the Englemann-Becker program, let me describe some of the critical ways in which paraprofessionals are helping that program in the Ocean Hill-Brownsville District of New York City. Paraprofessionals teach basic subject matter in reading, writing, and arithmetic. They are given two weeks of training before the school year starts, and most importantly, the academic material is very well outlined so that the presentation of materials—prompts, questions, sequencing of material— is standardized. In short, if a paraprofessional can read, he can present the material to the children so that children taught by the trained paraprofessional throughout the year can read as well as the children who are taught by the regular teacher who uses the same format and academic materials. That is, children from economically deprived areas learn to read at grade level whether they are taught by the regular teacher (a college graduate with professional certification) or by the teacher aide (a high school graduate with specific training) (Jackie Rogers, personal communication, Ocean Hill-Brownsville, New York, Head Start Follow-Through Program, December, 1970). What should be emphasized here is that when paraprofessionals are given adequate training they can definitely perform their functions well—in fact, almost, if not equally, as well as the "professional."

PEERS

The peer is an untapped source of great human potential in the schools. In contrast to the adult paraprofessional described before, I am here referring to programs in which a student is used to tutor another student who is his own age or one or two years his junior. The peer is even less frequently utilized in schools than the adult paraprofessional, but there are indications that his role, like that of the adult paraprofessional, may be increasing. As mentioned earlier, if one views the teaching process as a hierarchical one, there is no reason why children cannot teacher other children who are younger than themselves, but also there is little reason why one child could not teach another child who is his own age or relatively close to his age.

Surratt, Ulrich, and Hawkins (1969) had fifth grade students monitor the study behavior of four first grade students. Lights were placed on the desks of each of the four children and could be activated by the fifth grader who had a console controlling the four lights. Through a series of manipulations, Surratt *et al.* (1969) were able to show that when the fifth grader monitored the first graders, the study behavior of the first graders increased, and it increased particularly when the "lights" were essentially a token for a privilege. That is, if the child's light were on for a long enough period of time (for a large portion of a 20-minute period), the child could engage in an activity of his choice such as going to the gym or to the playground or performing janitorial tasks around the building. The fifth grade monitor had his own token economy in his classroom, and if he were allowed to operate the console, his teachers had to report that his academic performance was at least average. Fortunately, his work never went below average. Variations of the peer monitor procedure are not hard to envision. Peers could record all sorts of behavior, e.g., remaining in seat, being quiet, number of problems completed, etc. Peers could relieve teachers of classroom management duties so that the teachers could spend more time giving individual attention to specific children and more time instructing.

One variation of peer monitoring was reported by Winnett, Richards, Krasner, & Krasner (1971) in a "normal" second grade classroom. Here the children dispensed tokens to other children in a class of 25 children. Undergraduate students served as observers who recorded attending behavior of five target children, though the token program was in effect for all children. During this time the teacher was conducting individual reading, and she was not easily able to supervise or monitor the behavior of the rest of the class. The child monitor changed from one day to the next, but if a child were the monitor, he received the maximum number of tokens that were earned that day (7 or 8)—as did the children who were reading with the teacher. The monitor randomly circulated around the room during the 20-minute reading period, and if a child were reading, the monitor would place a token (a poker chip) in the child's token box (milk container) that the child kept next to him. To make sure that the children understood what they were to do, the teacher modeled the dispensing of tokens before the program began and role-played the token dispensing with the children. After the reading period the teacher recorded the number of tokens each child earned, and twice a week the children could buy a variety of goods on display in the classroom. The tokens were worth approximately one penny so that the children could buy relatively inexpensive items with the tokens (children were free to buy or save).

During the baseline determination the target children attended 41% of the recorded intervals. Two sets of observations taken on the third day and the seventh day of the child-monitored token programs indicated that the five target children were attending 62 and 67% of the intervals, respectively. This demonstration, as the authors aptly pointed out, was not done to show that a token program could increase attending but rather to demonstrate that second grade children could monitor and maintain their own program with minimal supervision. The authors also aptly pointed out that instead of prizes worth money, they could have used access to special activities as reinforcers.

In a study in progress at our laboratory school at Stony Brook, we have been investigating the effects of self-evaluation and peer-evaluation in first grade children. These children were referred to us because of deficiencies in academic or social behavior. Our general aim has been to determine how children can control their own social behavior with minimal teacher attention. That is, we would like to see if we can have children monitor and control the behavior of themselves and their peers so that the teacher can focus largely on academic pursuits. Since the symposium here concerns the use of paraprofessionals, I will focus only on the peer evaluation aspects of our work.

Peer evaluation consisted of having each child take a turn sitting in the front of the room monitoring the behavior of the rest of the class. During this time, the teacher worked individually with children on reading and language assignments. The child monitor or evaluator would watch certain behaviors of his peers, such as remaining in his seat, and he would rate each child on a 1-to-3 scale during a 15-minute period. For example, a child might get a 3 for being in his seat throughout the 15-minute period. He might get a 2 if he got out of his seat twice. He might get a 1 if he were out of his seat more than two times. The peer monitor recorded the in-seat behavior on a piece of paper on each child's desk. Throughout the study, the teacher's behavior was recorded, and she was asked to hold her behavior relatively constant across conditions. For example, she was asked to hold the frequency of her praise constant across all experimental conditions. The teacher did not give feedback to the monitor about the accuracy of his evaluations. To our surprise, in the absence of any back-up reinforcer for receiving a high or low rating, peer evaluations were associated with a reduction in disruptive behavior. That is, as peers evaluated a certain disruptive behavior, the disruptive behavior declined. Then as the peers evaluated another disruptive behavior, that disruptive behavior declined. In addition, however, disruptive behaviors that were not evaluated also frequently declined. It is possible that because of existing relationships among some of the disruptive behaviors, such a result should be expected. For example, if a child is in his seat, it is less likely that he will be hitting another child. On the other hand, because of the repeated results in the behavior modification literature that indicate that effects are very specific to the behavior being treated, we see these results as very promising but as ones we want to replicate before saying that peer evaluation alone was the critical factor responsible for the behavior change. However, if such results can be obtained in other classes and with different teachers, we feel we will have realized our aim of teaching children to control each other's behavior so that the teacher can focus *largely* on academic pursuits. I emphasize "largely" since one of the biggest problems we have encountered is overevaluation, which will have to be corrected by teacher feedback. That is, the children consistently overevaluate their peers. In addition, there is some bargaining and occasional vindictiveness on the part of the children. For example, we hear "you give me a 3, and I'll give you a 3." If a child monitor gives another child a 1 (the lowest rating) the recipient of the 1 may later give that child a 1 regardless of how he behaved. Thus despite the apparent effectiveness of the peer evaluation procedure, it is not without its problems, and some teacher intervention is required. As an attempt to deal with such problems as overevaluation and simultaneously minimizing teacher involvement, we plan to have the teacher randomly and unobtrusively observe one child in the class during every monitoring period and praise the monitor when his rating matches the teacher's rating. Ultimately, we hope to create a climate that will foster honest ratings, reduce bargaining, and require minimal teacher effort. In order to eliminate ratings that are unduly harsh or unduly lenient, one might also have the evaluator be an elected position. Phillips, Bailey, and Wolf (1969) found that having an elected manager or monitor who was allowed to both give and take away points in a token program in a cottage setting was not only an effective method of increasing the work behavior of juvenile offenders, it was also a highly preferred system.

The Soviet Union has certainly harnessed the aid of children in teaching other children both social and academic skills. As reported by Bronfenbrenner (1970) children in the Soviet Union are reared by the collective. Following the teachings of Makarenko, the child is to be brought up "in the collective, by the collective, and for the collective." Critical to this system is the emphasis on altruism and "socialist" competition. Competition extends into a host of activities including sports, service projects, personal grooming, and moral conduct. As is noted, however,

> Since each child's status depends in part on the standing of the collective of which
> he is a member, it is to each pupil's enlightened self-interest to watch over his
> neighbor, encourage the other's good performance and behavior, and help him
> when he is in difficulty. In this system the child's collective becomes the agent of
> adult society and the major sources of reward and punishment [p. 50].

The altruism is seen not only as helping individuals but more in the sense of "group adoption," where each class takes on responsibility for the upbringing of a group of children at a lower level. The older class might "adopt" a first grade and take responsibility for seeing that the first graders were escorted to school. They would teach them games, read to them, help them with homework, etc.

Whether one agrees with the specific ideology of the Soviet system or not, it seems that they have harnessed the aid of peers to help in both academic and social matters in a much more systematic way than is evidenced in other countries. The child-monitored and child-teacher systems have very distinct advantages, and they seem to offer an interesting method of teaching a child to pay closer attention not only to others' behavior but also to his own behavior. In addition, they might well be run on a democratic basis, and altruism could be emphasized heavily. In such a manner not only would there be training in self-government and self-management, but there also would be the decided advantage of having extra teachers (i.e., child-teachers) in the room.

SUMMARY

As has been demonstrated, we hope, the entrée of the adult paraprofessional and the peer into the classroom is highly desired. Whether used separately or in combination, their skills have been put to good use and the evaluations of their effectiveness would certainly seem to justify their continued service. In fact, the maintenance of a program after the initial effect has been demonstrated is one good criterion for its efficacy. On that count, the use of paraprofessionals and peers has certainly been clear. Schools where they have been in use request them more and more. (See Act 2725-A, State of New York, January 28, 1970.) Furthermore, as documented by Sobey (1970), of the 185 projects involving paraprofessionals in 1968 that were funded by NIMH:

> Almost half of the terminated projects became part of on-going projects of their
> sponsoring agency. One-fifth of the projects became part of the on-going program
> of another agency in the community . . . and in a few cases the entire sponsoring
> agency program was revamped as a result of the projects experiences.

In the long run it definitely appears that any disadvantages of the peers and paraprofessionals are far outweighed by their advantages, and the entrée of the peer and paraprofessional into the schools will soon be an accomplished fact.

From what I know of the educational system in Mexico, it would appear that because of the pupil-teacher ratio, the paraprofessional would be a decided advantage to the school system. However, because of some threats to a teacher's prestige and because of the general absence of a career ladder to accommodate a paraprofessional, I would recommend that local projects involving paraprofessionals might be initiated with peers and *volunteer* paraprofessionals. As their efficacy is demonstrated, the paraprofessional will then be *sought* by teachers, not seen as a threat to them. At that point, training for paraprofessionals or behavioral technicians might well be done at the second level similar to the technicians' level training now available in Mexico.

ACKNOWLEDGMENT

Special thanks goes to Ruth Kass and Susan O'Leary for their critical reading of this manuscript.

REFERENCES

Bandura, A., & Walters, R. H. *Social learning and personality development.* New York: Holt, Rinehart, & Winston. 1963.

Becker, W. C., Madsen, C. H., Arnold, C. R., & Thomas, D. R. The contingent use of teacher attention and praise in reducing classroom behavior problems. *Journal of Special Education,* 1967, **1**, 287-307.

Bijou, S. W., & Baer D. M. *Child Development:* Vol. 1 New York: Appleton-Century-Crofts, 1961.

Bronfenbrenner, U. *Two worlds of childhood: U.S. and U.S.S.R.* New York: Russell Sage Foundation, 1970.

Cloward, R. D. Studies in tutoring. *The Journal of Experimental Education*, 1967, **36**(1), 14-25.

Holt, J. *How children fail.* New York: Pitman Publ. Corp., 1964.

Nyquist, E. B. Nyquist backs British informal schooling plan. *New York Times*, December 8, 1970, p. 1.

O'Leary, K. D., & O'Leary, S. G. *Classroom management: The successful use of behavior modification.* New York: Pergamon, 1972.

Phillips, E. L., Bailey, J., & Wolf, M. M. Achievement place: A token economy in a home-style rehabilitation program for juvenile offenders. Paper presented to the American Psychological Association, Washington, D. C., 1969.

Ryback, D., & Staats, A. W. Parents as behavior therapy-technicians in treating reading deficits (dyslexia). *Journal of Behavior Therapy and Experimental Psychiatry*, 1970, **1**, 109-119.

Silberman, C. E. *Crisis in the classroom: The remaking of American education.* New York: Random House, 1970.

Skinner, B. F. Contingency management in the classroom. *Education*, 1969, **90**(2), 93-100.

Sobey, F. *The nonprofessional revolution in mental health.* New York: Columbia Univ. Press, 1970.

Staats, A. W., & Butterfield, W. H. Treatment of nonreading in a culturally deprived juvenile delinquent: An application of reinforcement principles. *Child Development*, 1965, **36**, 925-942.

Surratt, P. R., Ulrich, R. E., & Hawkins, R. P. An elementary student as a behavioral engineer. *Journal of Applied Behavior Analysis*, 1969, **2**, 85-92.

Tharp, R. G., & Wetzel, R. J. *Behavior modification in the natural environment.* New York: Academic Press, 1969.

Thomas, D. R., Nielson, L., Kuypers, D. S., & Becker, W. C. Social reinforcement and remedial instruction in the elimination of a classroom behavior problem. *The Journal of Special Education*, 1968, **2**, 291-305.

Ullmann L. P., & Krasner, L. *Case studies in behavior modification.* New York: Holt, Rinehart, & Winston, 1965.

Ulrich, R. E., Louisell, S. E., & Wolfe, M. The learning village: A behavioral approach to early education. *Educational Technology*, 1972, 12(3).

Wahler, R. G. Setting generality: Some specific and general effects of child behavior therapy. *Journal of Applied Behavior Analysis*, 1969, 2, 239-246.

Winnett, R. A., Richards, C. S., Krasner, M., & Krasner, L. Child-monitored token reading program. *Psychology in the Schools*, 1971, 3(3), 259-262.

Discussion: The Role of Teachers and Paraprofessionals in the Classroom

RODOLPHO CARBONARI SANT'ANNA

In his paper, O'Leary presented two kinds of arguments—political/financial and empirical. Our discussion will center around the empirical, namely, the use of teachers and paraprofessionals trained to apply behavioral techniques in the classroom situation.

A paraprofessional is any individual working in association with a person possessing a certain academic degree or professional certification by the State. In a classroom, the teacher is the professional; the paraprofessional is any other person working with her. The paraprofessional we are talking about is not merely an aide; she (or he) must be an aide trained in behavior modification techniques.

Initially we may ask: To what extent is it appropriate to use paraprofessionals to help solve the problems faced by almost all educational systems? These problems, despite certain regional features, have much in common: shortcomings in the instructional programs, the need for more school personnel, lack of instructional materials and specialized teachers, insufficient budgets, protests against increased duties for teachers, high percentage of student dropouts, etc. As an example of the crying need for improvement in the schools, we learn that in the state of Veracruz, 31% of the students in the Federal school system and

22% in the State school system repeat the first grade. For the second, third, fourth, fifth, and sixth grades, the repeat percentages are 33.8, 43.25, 53.66, 60.9, and 66.62, respectively. In Brazil, when the general enrollment in the first grade in 1959 and the actual enrollment in the fourth grade in 1962 are compared, the figures show that only 20% of those students enrolled in 1959 reached the fourth grade in 1962. Therefore, 80% dropped out or failed, or both, during that period (Pinheiro, 1966). These problems of school attrition, which are similar in various respects, may have different causes. Before an attempt is made to use the paraprofessional to help solve them, it is appropriate to take into account the causes maintaining these problems.

Let us examine some of the arguments presented by O'Leary concerning paraprofessionals. In considering the teacher's requests for paraprofessionals, we must think first about the teacher's own role in the school situation. From the learning viewpoint, the teacher should be the professional capable of manipulating the school environment and, it is hoped, the extracurricular situation as well, in order to promote the students' acquisition of particular behavioral repertoires. This means that the teacher must be trained in the use of behavior modification techniques. At present, this kind of training is virtually nonexistent.

Typical of teacher training in Mexico is the curriculum of the Normal School "Enrique C. Rebsamen" in Xalapa, which includes such courses as General Psychology, Psychology of Learning, Science of Education, Educational Psychology, Knowledge of the Pupil, and Pedagogical Psychotechnique and School Observation, each one comprising six hours per week during one semester and Techniques for Teaching, which covers 10, 10, and 12 hours per week during the second, third, and fourth years, respectively. The elementary teaching degree is generally obtained in three or four years, depending upon the course load a student chooses to carry. In addition, this Normal School has some adjoining facilities: a primary school (570 pupils) and a kindergarten (180 children), which, due to their experimental nature, "serve a chief role in the development of preparatory activities for school practicum." Presently, 988 students are enrolled in the Normal School. The mean annual number of students finishing the complete curriculum is approximately 250, most of whom are placed in the Federal or State school systems.

We believe that teachers should be trained not only in the usual subject matter of the Normal School but also in the use of behavioral techniques. Such additional specialized training can be justified in a number of ways. (1) It is easier to carry out a training program directed to a larger number of people rather than on an individual basis, which is now the case; (2) the present Normal School system already has the necessary facilities and experimental schools; (3) the students spend three or four years in the Normal School and hence have adequate time to study the principles of applied behavior analysis; (4) upon receiving the degree, a teacher could be assigned to a school for practical supervised experience with emphasis on her ability to apply behavioral techniques in the classroom. Her new status as a salaried teacher with an opportunity for promotion within the school system would provide the needed control of her performance. It seems, therefore, that the most economical way of altering the school environment is by properly training the teacher. The studies cited by O'Leary (Hall, Lund, & Jackson, 1968; Madsen, Becker, and Thomas, 1968) are two of the many examples of training teachers in behavior modification techniques.

The question next arises as to what kinds of techniques should be taught. The empirical solution to this question lies in the systematic observation of student-teacher interactions, since these interactions may be affected by economic and cultural factors, and also in comparative studies of the effectiveness of techniques created for the local setting with which we are concerned. This would constitute the basis for training programs. Independently of the kinds of programs to be used, the main objective must be the modification of the teacher's own behavior, rather than merely reading about or talking about the principles or techniques of behavior modification.

Another aspect of the training program is the selection of reinforcers that will be effective in maintaining the teacher's behavior. No doubt observation of the school environment and the mechanics of the system would point to some potential reinforcers. For example, assuming that a teacher would welcome the assistance of a paraprofessional, the assignment of this helper could be made contingent upon the teacher's prior performance of certain behaviors.

As stated earlier, our view is that the professional—the teacher—is the most adequate person for using applied behavior techniques in the classroom. The most economical solution would be to include this specialized training in the curriculum of the Normal School. This early Normal School training would not, of course, affect necessary parallel programs for retraining teachers already in the school system, some of whom do not have teaching degrees. In the state of Veracruz, for example, 29% of the primary school teachers do not have a degree. In Brazil, 32% of the teachers have only an elementary school education (Pinheiro, 1966). In order to facilitate the acceptance of behavior modification techniques in the school systems, a program of enlightenment and education in these techniques should be directed toward the administrative personnel, with their accepted authority.

THE EXTENSION OF THE BEHAVIOR PROGRAM

Generally, a child spends 20 hours a week in the school environment. To what extent can we expect the manipulation of the student's classroom behavior to affect his behavior outside the classroom? If it is true that the two situations are functionally independent in relation to the student's behavior, it seems logical to program specific contingencies for each setting. The more extensive a program is in terms of the number of variables manipulated, the greater will be the control developed. Here, the use of the paraprofessional to facilitate the extension of control may be indispensable. However, it is more realistic to assume that the generalization of behavior must be attempted in a procedure implemented in the classroom. There are problems regarding the effectiveness of such an extension procedure, since it could range from being consistent with "what behaviors in what settings must be modified in order to effect general changes in setting function [Wahler, 1969, p. 246]," to being quite indefinite.

DATA FROM ELEMENTARY SCHOOLS IN XALAPA

N. R. Toral (1970, personal communication) has obtained data relevant to the topic with which we are dealing. The subjects were 29 first grade, low-achieving children attending the primary demonstration school of the Normal School "Enrique C. Rebsamen" in Xalapa. Four behavior categories were observed: (1) study behaviors, (2) aggressive behaviors, (3) verbalization not related to the classroom task, and (4) other behaviors (standing up without permission, playing with objects, etc.). The data showed that only 51.8% of the total observations were in the category of study behaviors. This is in line with the finding that the normal child attends to his task in the classroom 77% of the overall time, whereas the disruptive child does so only 53% of the time (Werry & Quay, 1969). The low percentage of study behaviors (51.8%) of Toral's group may be directly related to their lack of academic skills. However, the teacher's evaluation of the students is especially perplexing. Her subjective estimates of the percentages of study behaviors were 44.4 and 47.8% for the two highest academic achievers, and 63.8, 56.2, and 51% for the three lowest achievers. This raises some serious questions. Is the teacher's judgment about who is a good or bad student in error? Or is the percentage of study behaviors not functionally related to academic achievement in the present classroom structure? Such would seem to be the case when a student with only 44% study behaviors is judged to be among the highest in academic achievement.

Other data were taken from several elementary school classes in Xalapa, in which the teacher's verbal behavior was directed to students seated in different parts of the classroom, i.e., in the front, middle, or back of the classroom. The data showed that only 22% of the teacher's verbal behavior was directed to the students in the back of the classroom, while the rest was devoted to the students sitting closer to her. Further, only 3% of the teacher's verbal behavior was classed as "approval behavior" (Pelaez, 1971, personal communication). This forces us to consider the physical arrangement of the classroom in terms of its effect on the behavior of both the students and the teacher. Facilitating student-teacher interactions, however, does not guarantee improvement in the school situation if the teacher is not able to use interactions effectively.

Another program, in the Nursery School "Gaston Melo" in Xalapa, was aimed at developing attending behaviors in a classroom of twelve children, five to seven years old. It was found that when a typical elementary school teacher trained at the Normal School was in charge, the attending behaviors were 54%; when an advanced psychology student with training in behavior modification techniques was in control, the level of attending behaviors reached 90% (Speller, 1970, personal communication). This again illustrates the need for teachers to be taught to become facile in the use of behavioral techniques.

EDUCATION CONCEIVED AS A HIERARCHICAL PROCESS

Our discussion has been focused on the need for training teachers rather than other paid paraprofessionals or volunteers. Nevertheless, we do not object to the use of paraprofessionals, provided that the teachers are well trained. The paraprofessional may work as a mediator of contingencies and the teacher as a behavior analyst, in accordance with the model of Tharp and Wetzel (1970). The practice of using paraprofessionals as contingency managers is dependent upon the development of group control techniques in which the students themselves act as contingency managers. The concept of education as a hierarchical process is closely related to the benefits that arise when students act as tutors of other students, even without being aware of behavior modification techniques. These techniques have been demonstrated to be effective at practically all levels of education.

REFERENCES

Hall, R. V., Lund, D., & Jackson, D. Effects of teacher attention on study behavior. *Journal of Applied Behavior Analysis*, 1968, 1, 1-12.

Madsen, C. H., Jr., Becker, W. C., & Thomas, D. R. Rules, praise, and ignoring: Elements of elementary classroom controversy. *Journal of Applied Behavior Analysis*, 1968, 1, 139-150.

Pinheiro, L. M. Treinamento, Formacao e Aperfeicoamento de professores primarios e o plano Nacional de Educacao. *Revista Brasileira de Estudios Pedagogicos*, 1966, 103, 8-64.

Tharp, R. G., & Wetzel, R. J. *Behavior modification in the natural environment*. New York: Academic Press, 1970.

Wahler, R. G. Setting generality: Some specific and general effects of child behavior therapy. *Journal of Applied Behavior Analysis*, 1969, 2(4), 239-246.

Werry, J. F., & Quay, H. C. Observing the classroom behavior of elementary school children. *Exceptional Children*, 1969, 35, 461-470.

GENERAL REFERENCES

La Educacion Publica en Mexico. Reporte de la Secretaria de Educacion Publica, 1964-67.

La Tecnica de la Ensenanza: Experiencia, Critica, Sugestiones. Paper presented by tne Escuela Normal Veracruzana "Enrique C. Rebsamen" in the IV National Meeting on Normal Education, Saltillo, Mexico, March, 1969.

New Roles for the Paraprofessional

TEODORO AYLLON and PATRICIA WRIGHT

The inability of present mental health programs to meet the needs of the people has long been recognized.

> The poor, the dispossessed, the uneducated, the 'poor treatment risk,' get less service . . . than their representation in the community warrants. . . . The more advanced mental health services have tended to be a middle-class luxury; chronic hospital custody a lower-class horror. . . . Most of our therapeutic talent . . . has been invested not in solving our hard-core mental health problem . . . but in treating the relatively well-to-do educated neurotic [Smith & Hobbs, 1969].

The current one-to-one, therapist-patient relationship is an inadequate tool for dealing with the mental health problems of our time. Further, current projections for training in the mental health professions indicate that demands for services will outstrip trained personnel in the foreseeable future (Hobbs, 1969). We must find new ways of utilizing our professional manpower and knowledge in order to make effective mental health services available to all of the people. As a result, it is necessary that the professionals train paraprofessional personnel to implement procedures for therapy and rehabilitation.

To meet this end, "therapy must be couched in a set of objective techniques which can be easily taught and implemented by relatively untrained personnel [Ayllon & Haughton, 1964]." Behavior modification techniques meet this criteria.

This approach regards behavior as being governed by its consequences. Behavior cannot then, be understood independent of the environment within which it occurs. Any attempts at changing the behavior of an individual, therefore, must be aimed at altering the environmental contingencies.

To modify behavior, it is necessary to concentrate (1) on the stimulus situations in which the behavior is most likely to be emitted and (2) on the consequences following the behavior. In the case of the hospital patient, it is primarily the ward attendants who arrange the patient's environment and provide consequences for behavior. In the case of the child, it is primarily the parents who set up the behavior contingencies at home.

A technology of behavior is now at hand. Research and application of principles of behavior have been extended to include paraprofessionals as the agents of change. The paraprofessional personnel represent a new means of delivering care and assistance to three major types of social settings: the mental and correctional institutions, the school, and the home. The paraprofessional personnel cover a wide range in (1) age—from a twelve-year-old child to adults, (2) education—from a fifth grader to college graduates, and (3) professional role—from volunteer, unpaid mothers to paid, staff personnel.

WHAT ARE THE TARGET BEHAVIORS?

What types of problems have professionals worked with? What are the target behaviors toward which they have worked? In each of the three settings, the mental and correctional institutions, the school, and the home, the target behaviors can be roughly divided into eliminating undesirable behaviors and producing and maintaining desirable behaviors.

Initially, in working with hospitalized mental patients, the emphasis was placed on symptomatic behaviors because they are observable, specific, and measurable. In the literature, paraprofessional personnel have been reported to have eliminated the stealing of food (Ayllon, 1963), the hoarding of towels (Ayllon, 1963), the wearing of too many clothes (Ayllon, 1963), and symptomatic verbal behavior (Ayllon & Haughton, 1964) in adult patients. In working with a hospitalized autistic child, Jensen and Womack (1967) decreased or eliminated stereotyped autistic behavior, tantrum behavior, abusive behavior, and excessively aggressive behavior.

In time, the elimination of symptomatic behavior can prove to be a sometimes inadequate and insufficient approach. Often patients emit so many of these behaviors that their elimination would involve too much time and effort. Even if all these behaviors were eliminated, no positive results would have been produced. Instead, a second and more positive approach works to "facilitate the patient's rehabilitation by making him a responsible, functioning human being [Ayllon, 1971]." Studies have dealt with producing and maintaining various target behaviors with adult hospitalized mental patients: social responses between patients (Ayllon & Haughton, 1962), physical activity (Ayllon & Haughton, 1962; Winkler, 1970), attendance at activities (Ayllon & Azrin, 1968a), and normal eating behavior (Ayllon & Haughton, 1962). In addition, paraprofessionals have produced such self-help behaviors as self-feeding, handwashing, dressing, bathing, toileting, etc. (Panyan, Boozer, & Morris, 1970; Winkler, 1970) and toilet training (Wolf, Risley, Johnston, Harris, & Allen, 1964). Jensen and Womack (1967) produced peer interaction, cooperative play, and an increased use of language and names in an autistic child. Paraprofessionals (Ayllon & Azrin, 1968b) have also produced and maintained attendant-like behavior in hospitalized mental patients. This allows the patients to maintain the functioning of the hospital environment and maintains the functioning of the patient at as "maximal [a] level as he would have to [have] upon return to the outside world. . . ."

> The major objective of the hospital of tomorrow should be to generate in the patients a desire to rejoin the human family by way of acquiring skills with which to maintain themselves after their release [Ayllon, 1971].

In the correctional setting, work has been done to eliminate "undesirable" behaviors. The institutional staff has eliminated antisocial behavior (Burchard & Tyler, 1965) and misbehavior in the poolroom (Tyler & Brown, 1967) in delinquents.

In the school setting, the first effort by paraprofessionals was to eliminate certain specific, observable, and measurable behaviors that were considered undesirable. A nursery school staff (Wolf et al., 1964) reduced stereotyped autistic behavior in a four-year-old autistic boy. Studies have stated various other target behaviors to be eliminated in the school setting: isolate behavior (Harris, Wolf, & Baer, 1964b), excessively withdrawn behavior (Ward & Baker, 1968), resistive behavior (Wasik, Senn, Welch, & Cooper, 1969), regressive behaviors such as baby talk (Zimmerman & Zimmerman, 1962) and crawling (Harris, Johnston, Kelley, & Wolf, 1964a), excessive crying (Harris et al., 1964b; Hart, Reynolds, Baer, Brawley, & Harris, 1968), excessively passive behavior (Harris et al., 1964b), tantrum behavior (Davison, 1965; Zimmerman & Zimmerman, 1962), and excessively aggressive behavior (Brown & Elliott, 1965; Wasik et al., 1969). In addition, many studies have dealt with eliminating inappropriate classroom behaviors (O'Leary & Becker, 1967), i.e., those behaviors which compete with and hinder learning. More specifically, these include disruptive behaviors (Bushell, Wrobel, & Michalis, 1968; Hall, Panyan, Rabon, & Broden, 1968b; Madsen, Becker, & Thomas, 1968; McAllister, Stachowiak, Baer, & Conderman, 1969; O'Leary, Becker, Evans, & Saudergas, 1969; Thomas, Becker, & Armstrong, 1968; Ward & Baker, 1968; Williams, 1959; Winkler, 1970; Zimmerman & Zimmerman, 1962), out-of-seat behavior (Osborne, 1962), and excessive noise (Schmidt & Ulrich, 1969).

Paraprofessionals, in the school setting, have also worked to produce and maintain several types of target behaviors: social-interactional behaviors, behaviors for autistic children, motor skills, behaviors that are necessary for a "learning" atmosphere, and specific academic skills. Two types of social-interactional behaviors have been produced: peer interaction (Allen, Henke, Harris, Baer, & Reynolds, 1967) and cooperative play (Hart et al., 1968; Hart, Allen, Buell, Harris, & Wolf, 1964). Martin, England, Kaprowy, Kilgour, & Pelik (1968) trained autistic children to function as a group in a kindergarten class, and Davison (1964; 1965) trained autistic children to obey commands. Motor skills have been improved through increasing motor play (Buell, Stoddard, Harris, & Baer, 1968) and physical activity (Johnston, Kelley, Harris, & Wolf, 1966). Many studies have dealt with producing the classroom behaviors that are necessary for a "learning" atmosphere, i.e., an environment that is conducive to learning: (1) increasing attending behavior (Allen & Harris, 1966; Jacobsen, Bushell, & Risley, 1969; Madsen et al., 1968; Packard, 1970; Ward & Baker, 1968; Osborne, 1962) and (2) increasing study behavior (Bushell et al., 1968; Hall, Lund, & Jackson, 1968a; Suratt, Ulrich, & Hawkins, 1969; Thomas et al., 1968). In addition, much paraprofessional work has aimed at improving specific academic skills. Included are increasing spelling accuracy (Lovitt, Gupp, & Blattner, 1969; Evans & Oswalt, 1968; Zimmerman & Zimmerman, 1962), improving verbal skills (Dreitzer, 1969; Reynolds & Risley, 1968; Risley & Hart, 1968), improving reading ability (Ryback & Staats, 1970), and increasing academic achievement (Wolf, Giles, & Hall, 1968).

In the home setting, parents have worked to eliminate specific, observable, and measurable symptomatic and "undesirable" social-interactional behaviors. Included have been excessive scratching (Allen and Harris, 1966) and tantrum behavior (Hawkins, Peterson, Schweid, & Bijou, 1966; O'Leary, O'Leary, & Becker, 1967; Williams, 1959). In addition, paraprofessionals have eliminated inadequate and "undesirable" ways of social interaction: isolate behavior (O'Leary et al., 1967), excessively dependent behavior (Wahler, Winkel, Peterson, & Morrison, 1965), commanding behavior (Wahler et al., 1965), defiance (Shah, 1969), negativism (Russo, 1964), abusive behavior (Russo, 1964), disobedience (Hawkins et al., 1966; Shah, 1969), oppositional behavior (Wahler, 1969; Wahler et al., 1965), and excessively aggressive behavior (O'Leary et al., 1967; Ryback & Staats, 1970; Shah, 1969; Wahler et al., 1965; Zeilberger, Sampen, & Sloane, 1968).

Parents have produced and maintained cooperative play (O'Leary et al., 1967; Wahler et al., 1965) and improved bowel control in a 5½-year-old child (Barrett, 1969).

In summary, paraprofessionals have worked toward target behaviors in three settings—the mental and correctional institutions, the school, and the home. These behaviors are all observable, specific, and measurable. In addition, they have aimed at eliminating undesirable symptomatic behaviors as well as producing behaviors that are functional and will continue to be maintained by the environment.

HOW ARE PARAPROFESSIONALS TRAINED?

What type of information is given and how is it disseminated? What training devices, if any, are used? How much time is involved in the training and how closely are the paraprofessional personnel supervised?

In general, the training program consists, singly or in combinations, of the following: (1) specific instructions, (2) lectures or training in the principles and theory of behavior modification, (3) demonstrations, (4) verbal feedback sessions, (5) cueing systems, (6) general discussion of aims and the procedural outline, (7) training on how to observe and record behavior, and (8) reading assignments. Paraprofessionals were trained both singly and in a group situation. Training was sometimes received on the job and sometimes as instructions that were to be applied in another setting, as the home.

The predominant training method used was specific instructions in the implementation of procedures. With this type of training method, the paraprofessional personnel carry out the environmental manipulation under the direction of the how, when, and where of responding to certain behaviors, such as "dismiss class immediately for recess if S spells word correctly or continue class if he does not [Evans & Oswalt, 1968]." Usually no explanation is given of reinforcement theory or the reasons that the procedure works. However, Ayllon and Haughton (1964) found that the staff's lack of knowledge regarding conditioning seemed to facilitate their following instructions. Thus, it is only necessary that the professional monitor the application of procedures and the recording of data, since the nonprofessional is often not interested in record keeping.

Specific instructions have been given to paraprofessionals who have previously been instructed in and applied the principles of behavior modification (Kreitzer, 1969; Packard, 1970; Wolf et al., 1964). Brown and Elliott, 1965) presented specific instructions accompanied by a very general explanation—i.e., "many fights occur because they bring with them . . . attention from adults."

Various studies have instructed paraprofessionals, emphasizing different aspects of the principles of behavior modification. Wasik et al., 1969 and Ward and Baker (1968) discussed the need to clearly and carefully define the behaviors required. It was stressed that behaviors should be responded to immediately (Ward and Baker, 1968; Wasik et al., 1969), consistently (Shah, 1969; Wahler, 1969; Ward & Baker, 1968; Wasik et al., 1969), and conscientiously (Shah, 1969). In addition, contingencies (Shah, 1969; Ward & Baker, 1968), schedules of reinforcement (Ward & Baker, 1968), primary and secondary reinforcement procedures (Davison, 1964; 1965; Ward & Baker, 1968), punishment procedures (Ward & Baker, 1968), functional relationships (Shah, 1969), differential reinforcement (Davison, 1965; Wahler, 1969), and the alternatives available when S is engaged in deviant behavior (Davison, 1965) were emphasized.

Davison (1964) demonstrated the many contingencies that could arise in the course of actual treatment as well as the procedure for accompanying primary reinforcement with a smile and praise followed by a remark that explained how the reinforcer had been earned. Ryback and Staats (1970) gave an outline, explanation, and demonstration of the procedures, after which questions were answered and the paraprofessionals practiced the procedures. O'Leary and Becker (1967) gave a week demonstration of the procedures of the token exchange period, followed by the teacher administering the procedure unaided. Russo's (1964) demonstration procedure involved a three-way interaction: First the mother observed the therapist as he worked with the child; next the mother began to take part, along with the child and the therapist; and when this process was satisfactorily underway, the therapist withdrew to observe.

Paraprofessionals were taught how to respond to specific behaviors through verbal feedback and cueing systems. Various studies used hand-gestural signals (Becker, Madsen, Arnold, & Thomas, 1967; Hawkins, Peterson, Schweid, & Bijou, 1966; O'Leary et al., 1967), cards with instructions written on them (Madsen et al., 1968), different colored squares of paper (Hall et al., 1968), and lights (Wahler et al., 1965; Ward & Baker, 1968) to teach discriminating responses and later to provide reinforcement to the paraprofessional for correct responses. Wahler et al., (1965) trained through instructions before sessions, light signals during, and feedback after sessions. Becker et al. (1967) attempted hand signals but found them too disruptive while teaching and so resorted to specific instructions and feedback sessions. Hall et al. (1968) trained his teachers through specific instructions and daily discussions of the observations made during the sessions. Teachers (Wasik et al., 1969) provided their own feedback on the effectiveness of their interactions by plotting the day-by-day changes in behavior. Graduate students observed and informed teachers of deviations from the instructions and reinforced appropriate responses. Feedback conferences were also used (Hall et al., 1968; McAllister et al., 1969; Russo, 1964) to provide praise, criticism, and suggestions to the paraprofessionals.

How much time is involved in the actual training of the paraprofessionals? O'Leary et al., (1967) gave one week of demonstrations on the operation of token-exchange. Panyan et al. (1970) taught a four-week course in the principles of operant conditioning. After obtaining the baseline measurement, Ward and Baker (1968) began a series of four weekly seminars on behavior modification and progress of the children. Davison (1965) and Ryback and Staats (1970) trained nonprofessionals in approximately four hours; in addition, Ryback and Staats (1970) conducted three, one-half-hour group meetings in an eight-week program to discuss specific behavior problems and problems of motivation. Hirsch and Walder (1969) conducted nine group meetings of one and one-half hours each over a five-week period. Wahler (1969) trained the parents of two boys to eliminate oppositional behavior in four sessions of 30-65 minutes each for one boy and seven sessions of 30-105 minutes each for the other. However, since most of the studies utilized such on-the-job training as specific instructions and feedback sessions, it is extremely difficult to determine the amount of training time.

How much professional supervision is necessary for the nonprofessional? As discussed previously, when only specific instructions are given, it is necessary that the professional monitor the execution of the procedures almost constantly. Even when the training is more extensive, professionals supervised the paraprofessionals and informed them of their effectiveness through feedback sessions (Becker *et al.,* 1967; McAllister *et al.,* 1969). Wahler (1969) gave instructions and helped the parent work with the child and then withdrew to watch and record for the second half of the session. In another study (Ryback & Staats, 1970), parents were supervised directly the first couple of weeks and then the professional withdrew and observed, using a checklist. Russo (1964) began working with the child, the mother then joined after observing and the interaction became three-way; after a while, the professional withdrew to observe and only rarely took part in the therapy. However, feedback was presented to the mother by way of conferences held after sessions. Other studies (Hawkins *et al.,* 1966; O'Leary *et al.,* 1967; Wahler *et al.,* 1965; Zeilberger *et al.,* 1968) have provided feedback by way of showing the teachers data obtained through observation. Wasik *et al.* (1969) taught their teachers to graph their own day-by-day changes in behavior, which made them better qualified to supervise their own behavior. Other studies (Allen & Harris, 1966; Davison, 1964; Hirsch & Walder, 1969; Shah, 1969) required that the paraprofessional keep detailed behavioral notes that enabled the professional to monitor their work.

HOW EFFECTIVE ARE PARAPROFESSIONAL THERAPISTS?

Many different types of paraprofessionals have been able to successfully alter behavior. Teachers can be taught behavior modification procedures and can use them to produce and maintain the desired target behaviors in students (Becker *et al.,* 1967; Bushell *et al.,* 1968; Hall *et al.,* 1968a; Hall *et al.,* 1968b; Wasik *et al.,* 1969). Davison (1964; 1965) found that undergraduate college students can acquire a significant degree of control over the behavior of psychotic children. A fifth grade student was trained to operate a light console, which successfully modified several children's behavior at one time (Suratt *et al.,* 1969). Parents (Hawkins *et al.,* 1966; Hirsch & Walder, 1969; O'Leary *et al.,* 1967; Russo, 1964; Wahler *et al.,* 1965; Zeilberger *et al.,* 1968) have effectively altered their children's behavior in the desired direction. A five-week follow-up (Hirsch & Walder, 1969) showed that the improved behaviors were maintained.

Paraprofessionals work more effectively in some situations and settings than is possible for professionals. Behavior changes of a child by his parents are more likely to be maintained than those changes made only by a therapist. Parental treatment processes can last all day, everyday, for as long as they are needed. With the parents as therapists, the treatment process may be preventative as well as corrective. Training teachers is a way of reaching children in a setting where direct observation and manipulation of behavior by a professional is not possible. In addition, the use of paraprofessionals from the three therapeutic settings—the home, the school, and mental and correctional institutions—has the advantage of providing a much lower therapist-patient ratio than would be possible if only professional personnel were used. The use of parents as paraprofessionals maximizes this advantage in that it provides the lowest patient-therapist ratio and yet still reaches the greatest number of people.

CONCLUSIONS

In summary, the literature on behavior modification has shown that parapro-fessionals, of a wide educational and age range, can be taught to effectively modify many types of behaviors for a wide range of patients. In addition, these paraprofessionals can work more effectively in some settings than can the professional.

What does this mean in terms of future behavioral intervention? Will the professional be replaced by paraprofessional personnel? The answer is *no*! What the paraprofessional personnel does is to effectively extend the reach and scope of professional services. The professional is still needed to analyze problems in performance or behavioral terms. In effect, he becomes a "trouble-shooter"—involved in refining and developing new procedures to suit the ever-changing characteristics of behavior, vis-à-vis the environment.

In the future, perhaps the advantages of paraprofessional personnel use can be multiplied through the use of an, until now, relatively untapped source of manpower, i.e., college students. They bring with them motivation and a growing number of them a knowledge of operant techniques and behavior modification procedures. Besides providing a wealth of experience for the students, it can further extend the skills of the professional. The student can become a link between the professional and paraprofessional. He can train, observe, record, and provide some help in the way of advice and feedback to the paraprofessional. In this way, the professional could be kept up-to-date on the treatment process with a minimum of on-the-scene monitoring.

Behavioral techniques need to be put to use where they are needed most: with human problems irrespective of age, educational background, or income. The rapid growth of paraprofessional services is a testimonial to the ease with which behavioral techniques can be taught to those concerned with human problems.

REFERENCES

Allen, K. E., & Harris, F. R. Elimination of a child's excessive scratching by training the mother in reinforcement procedures. *Behavior Research and Therapy*, 1966, 4, 79-84.

Allen, K. E., Henke, L. B., Harris, F. R., Baer, D. M., & Reynolds, N. J. Control of hyper-activity by social reinforcement of attending behavior. *Journal of Educational Psy-chology*, 1967, 58, 231-237.

Ayllon, T. Intensive treatment of psychotic behavior by stimulus satiation and food reinforcement. *Behavior Research and Therapy*, 1963, **1**, 53-61.

Ayllon, T. Toward a new hospital psychiatry. In G. Abrams and N. Greenfield (Eds.), *The New Hospital Psychiatry*, Academic Press, 1971.

Ayllon, T., & Azrin, N. H. Reinforcer sampling: A technique for increasing the behavior of mental patients. *Journal of Applied Behavior Analysis*, 1968, **1**, 13-20.   (a)

Ayllon, T., & Azrin, N. H. *The token economy: A motivational system for therapy and rehabilitation.* New York: Appleton, 1968.   (b)

Ayllon, T., & Haughton, E. Control of the behavior of schizophrenic patients by food. *Journal of the Experimental Analysis of Behavior*, 1962, **5**, 343-352.

Ayllon, T., & Haughton, E. Modification of symptomatic verbal behavior of mental patients. *Behavior Research and Therapy*, 1964, **2**, 87-97.

Barrett, B. H. Behavior modification in the home: parents adapt laboratory-developed tactics to bowel-train a 5½-year-old. *Psychotherapy: Theory, Research and Practice*, 1969, **6**, 172-176.

Becker, W. C., Madsen, C. H., Jr. Arnold, C. R., & Thomas, D. R. The contingent use of teacher attention and praise in reducing classroom behavior problems. *Journal of Special Education*, 1967, **1**, 287-307.

Brown, P., & Elliott, R. Control of Aggression in a nursery school class. *Journal of Experimental Child Psychology*, 1965, **2**, 103-107.

Buell, J., Stoddard, P. Harris, F. R., & Baer, D. M., Collateral social development accompanying reinforcement of outdoor play in a preschool child. *Journal of Applied Behavior Analysis*, 1968, **1**, 167-173.

Burchard, J., & Tyler, V. Jr. The modification of delinquent behavior through operant conditioning. *Behavior Research and Therapy*, 1965, **2**, 245-250.

Bushell, D., Jr., Wrobel, P. A. & Michaelis, M. L., Applying "group" contingencies to the classroom study behavior of preschool children. *Journal of Applied Behavior Analysis*, 1968, **1**, 55-61.

Davison, G. C. A social learning therapy programme with an autistic child. *Behavior Research and Therapy*, 1964, **2**, 149-159.

Davison, G. C. The training of undergraduates as social reinforcers for autistic children. In L. P. Ullman and L. Krasner (Eds.). *Case Studies in Behavior Modification.* New York: Holt, 1965.

Evans, G. W., & Oswalt, G. L. Acceleration of academic progress through the manipulation of peer influence. *Behavior Research and Therapy*, 1968, **6**, 189-195.

Hall, R. V., Lund, D. & Jackson, D., Effects of teacher attention on study behavior. *Journal of Applied Behavior Analysis*, 1968, **1**, 1-12.   (a)

Hall, R. V., Panyan, M., Rabon, D. & Broden, M., Instructing beginning teachers in reinforcement procedures which improve classroom control. *Journal of Applied Behavior Analysis*, 1968, **1**, 315-322.   (b)

Harris, F. R., Johnston, M. K., Kelley, C. S., & Wolf, M. M. Effects of social reinforcement on regressed crawling of a nursery school child. *Journal of Educational Psychology*, 1964, **55**, 35-41.   (a)

Harris, F. R., Wolf, M. M. & Baer, D. M., Effects of adult social reinforcement on child behavior. *Young Children*, 1964, **20**, 8-17.   (b)

Hart, B. M., Allen, K. E., Buell, J. S., Harris, F. R., & Wolf, M. M. Effects of social reinforcement on operant crying. *Journal of Experimental Child Psychology*, 1964, **1**, 145-153.

Hart, B. M., Reynolds, N. J. Baer, D. M., Brawley, E. R., & Harris, F. R., Effect of contingent and non-contingent social reinforcement on the cooperative play of a preschool child. *Journal of Applied Behavior Analysis*, 1968, **1**, 73-76.

Hawkins, R. P., Peterson, R. F., Schweid, E. & Bijou, S. W., Behavior therapy in the home: Amelioration of problem parent-child relations with the parent in a therapeutic role. *Journal of Experimental Child Psychology*, 1966, **4**, 99-107.

Hirsch, I., & Walder, L. Training mothers in groups as reinforcement therapists for their own children. Reprinted from the *Proceedings*, 77th Annual Convention, American Psychology Association, 1969.
Hobbs, N. Mental health's third revolution. In B. G. Guerney (Ed.), *Psychotherapeutic agents: New roles for nonprofessionals, parents, and teachers.* New York: Holt, 1969.
Jacobsen, J. M., Bushell, D. Jr., & Risley, T. Switching requirements in a Head Start classroom. *Journal of Applied Behavior Analysis*, 1969, 2, 43-47.
Jensen, G. & Womack, M. G. Operant conditioning techniques applied in the treatment of an autistic child. *American Journal of Orthopsychiatry*, 1967, 37, 30-34.
Johnston, M. K., Kelley, C. S., Harris, F. R., & Wolf, M. An application of reinforcement principles to development of motor skills of a young child. *Child Development*, 1966, 37, 379-387.
Kreitzer, S. F. College students in a behavior therapy program with hospitalized emotionally disturbed children. In B. G. Guerney (Ed.). *Psychotherapeutic Agents: New Roles for Nonprofessionals, Parents, and Teachers.* New York: Holt, 1969.
Lovitt, T. C., Guppy, T. E., & Blattner, J. E. The use of a free-time contingency with fourth graders to increase spelling accuracy. *Behavior Research and Therapy*, 1969, 7, 151-156.
Madsen, C. H. Jr., Becker, W. C., & Thomas, D. R. Rules, praise, and ignoring: elements of elementary classroom control. *Journal of Applied Behavior Analysis*, 1968, 1, 139-150.
Martin, G. L., England, G., Kaprowy, E., Kilgour, K., & Pelik, V. Operant conditioning of kindergarten-class behavior in autistic children. *Behavior Research and Therapy*, 1968, 6, 281-204.
McAllister, L. W., Stachowiak, J. G., Baer, D. M., & Conderman, L. The application of operant conditioning techniques in a secondary school classroom. *Journal of Applied Behavior Analysis*, 1969, 2, 277-285.
O'Leary, K. D., & Becker, W. C. Behavior modification of an adjustment class: A token reinforcement program. *Exceptional children*, 1967, 33, 637-642.
O'Leary, K. D., Becker, W. C., Evans, M. B., & Saudargas, R. A. A token reinforcement program in a public school: A replication and systematic analysis. *Journal of Applied Behavior Analysis*, 1969, 2, 3-13.
O'Leary, K. D., O'Leary, S., & Becker, W. C. Modification of a deviant sibling interaction pattern in the home. *Behavior Research and Therapy*, 1967, 5, 113-120.
Osborne, J. G. Free-time as a reinforcer in the management of classroom behavior. *Journal of Applied Behavior Analysis*, 1962, 2, 113-118.
Packard, R. G. The control of "classroom attention": A group contingency for complex behavior. *Journal of Applied Behavior Analysis*, 1970, 3, 13-28.
Panyan, M., Boozer, H., & Morris, N. Feedback to attendants as a reinforcer for applying operant techniques. *Journal of Applied Behavior Analysis*, 1970, 3, 1-4.
Reynolds, N. J., & Risley, T. R. The role of social and material reinforcers in increasing talking of a disadvantaged preschool child. *Journal of Applied Behavior Analysis*, 1968, 1, 253-262.
Risley, T. R., & Hart, B. Developing correspondence between the non-verbal and verbal behavior of preschool children. *Journal of Applied Behavior Analysis*, 1968, 1, 267-281.
Russo, S. Adaptations in behavioral therapy with children. *Behavior Research and Therapy*, 1964, 2, 43-47.
Ryback, D., & Staats, A. W. Parents as behavior therapy-technicians in treating reading deficits (Dyslexia). *Journal of Behavior Therapy and Experimental Psychiatry*, 1970, 1, 109-119.
Schmidt, G. W., & Ulrich, R. E. Effects of group contingent events upon classroom noise. *Journal of Applied Behavior Analysis*, 1969, 2, 171-179.
Shah, S. A. Training and utilizing a mother as the therapist for her child. In B. G. Guerney (Ed.), *Psychotherapeutic agents: New roles for nonprofessionals, parents, and teachers.* New York: Holt, 1969.

Smith, M. B., & Hobbs, N. The community and the community mental health center. In B. G. Guerney (Ed.), *Psychotherapeutic agents: New roles for nonprofessionals, parents, and teachers.* New York: Holt, 1969.

Suratt, P. R., Ulrich, R. E., & Hawkins, R. P., An elementary school student as a behavioral engineer. *Journal of Applied Behavior Analysis,* 1969, 2, 85-92.

Thomas, D. R., Becker, W. C., & Armstrong, M., Production and elimination of disruptive classroom behavior by systematically varying teacher's behavior. *Journal of Applied Behavior Analysis,* 1968, 1, 35-45.

Tyler, V. O., & Brown, G. D. The use of swift, brief isolation as a group control device for institutionalized delinquents. *Behavior Research and Therapy,* 1967, 5, 1-9.

Wahler, R. G. Oppositional children: A quest for parental reinforcement control. *Journal of Applied Behavior Analysis,* 1969, 2, 159-170.

Wahler, R. G., Winkel, G. H., Peterson, R. F., & Morrison, D. C., Mothers as behavior therapists for their own children. *Behavior Research and Therapy,* 1965, 3, 113-124.

Ward, M. H., & Baker, B. L. Reinforcement therapy in the classroom. *Journal of Applied Behavior Analysis,* 1968, 1, 323-328.

Wasik, B. H., Senn, K., Welch, R. H., & Cooper, B. R. Behavior modification with culturally deprived school children: Two case studies. *Journal of Applied Behavior Analysis,* 1969, 2, 181-194.

Williams, C. D. The elimination of tantrum behavior by extinction procedures. *Journal of Abnormal and Social Psychology,* 1959, 59, 269.

Winkler, R. C. Management of chronic psychiatric patients by a token reinforcement system. *Journal of Applied Behavior Analysis,* 1970, 3, 47-55.

Wolf, M. M., Giles, D. K., & Hall, R. V. Experiments with token reinforcement in a remedial classroom. *Behavior Research and Therapy,* 1968, 6, 51-64.

Wolf, M., Risley, T., & Mees, H. Application of operant conditioning procedures to the behavior problems of an autistic child. *Behavior Research and Therapy,* 1964, 1, 305-312.

Zeilberger, J., Sampen, S. E., & Sloane, H. N. Modification of a child's problem behaviors in the home with the mother as therapist. *Journal of Applied Behavior Analysis,* 1968, 1, 47-53.

Zimmerman, E. H., & Zimmerman, J. The alteration of behavior in a special classroom situation. *Journal of the Experimental Analysis of Behavior,* 1962, 5, 59-60.

Discussion: A New Perspective:
Chronic Patients as Assistants
in a Behavior Rehabilitation Program
in a Psychiatric Institution

BENJAMIN DOMINGUEZ T., FELIPE ACOSTA N.,
AND DEMENTRIO CARMONA

There are, as has been pointed out (e.g., in the chapter by Ayllon and Wright) a number of problems concerning the participation of nonprofessional personnel in mental health programs. This presentation includes (1) a description of reinforcement procedures to solve some of these problems and (2) some possible perspectives for ameliorating a wide variety of human problems.

It is true that many professionals do not agree on the specific procedures used in mental health programs, but most do agree that rehabilitation programs are in urgent need of improvement. There are a variety of problems to be faced in psychiatric institutions: untrained personnel who reduce the effectiveness of mental health programs, the small number of professionals (psychiatrists, psychologists, social workers, nurses) relative to the number of patients, and the lack of supervision and inadequate wages that establish and maintain many antitherapeutic attitudes. Several authors have dealt with problems resulting from the mere fact of institutionalization (Goffman, 1961; Greenblatt, Levinson, & Williams, 1957), and alternatives have been posed (Dominguez, 1970; and Miron, 1968).

The need for new programs of proven efficiency in modifying the behavior of long-term institutionalized patients is becoming increasingly urgent. Recently, a new approach, based on an experimental analysis of behavior, has been used in a wide variety of behavioral problems (e.g., Ayllon & Azrin, 1968; Ulrich, Stachnick, & Mabry, 1970). It should be clear that the needed changes in institutions include not only the difficult task of going from predominantly custodial programs to rehabilitation-oriented ones but solving other pressing problems as well.

After dealing with many of the staff, supervision, and wage problems in psychiatric institutions, several investigators have undertaken treatment programs that involve the participation of the hospital employees (Ayllon, 1963; Ayllon & Azrin, 1968) and the training of the nurse personnel (Ayllon, 1963; Ayllon & Haughton, 1962, 1964; Ayllon & Michael, 1959). The possibility of employing the patients themselves as program assistants is a recent alternative (Hopkins, 1969, personal communication; Kale and Zlutnick, & Hopkins, 1968). This is the direction of our endeavor, which will be described next.

The country hospital, "Dr. Samuel Ramirez Moreno," under the Sanity and Assistance Secretary in Mexico, has a population of approximately 490 patients distributed among five wards. All of the patients with legal problems (about 95) are assigned to Ward 5, which consists of living quarters and a prison-like fenced yard. Ward 5, which has many of the problems typical of a penal institution, has the goal of rendering treatment and rehabilitation. The project, "Intensive Socialization," which was begun in October, 1969, is directed toward achieving improved social performance of patients inside the ward. This goal was selected for the following reasons.

1. In most cases, it could not be said that patients were being discharged as "cured."

2. The extreme behavioral deficits of many of the patients reduced the probability of their reintegration into the community, considering the demands of the community.

Ward 5 functions under the direction of a psychiatrist who is present for three hours a day, five days a week. There are approximately six caretakers during each of the three, eight-hour shifts. Their work includes the ward upkeep, administrative work, nursing tasks, and supervision of the patients. Obviously, the staff is small, and it would be quite difficult for the staff to undertake additional tasks such as the establishment of a behavior rehabilitation program utilizing tokens.

Faced with this limitation (not to mention the problem of financial support), one alternative was to quickly abandon the project. We did not do so, but proceeded instead to "invite" three patients from the ward to serve as observers. We began the training, which consisted mainly of instructions, supervision, and demonstrations by the psychiatrist himself. The specific task was to record behavior in 15-minute intervals using three categories of behavior. The objective in training was to have the behavior of the observers come under the control of the behavior of the subjects. A system of reliable behavior observations was established by making reinforcement for the three observers contingent upon the degree of similarity among their recordings. Reinforcement for the three patient-assistants was organized into a point system: they receive 2 points for each 15 minutes of recording, and from 3 to 5 points for the similarity among the recordings. The points can be exchanged every third day for such things as hair cream, American cigarettes, mechanical magazines, *Playboy* magazine, etc. The points and the date are recorded on cards which the patient-assistants carry with them.

The patient-assistants selected from an initial population of 16 "trouble makers" in the ward (i.e., those having high frequencies of fighting and stealing) were trained three at a time. They had in common the following.

1. All had been institutionalized for an average of nine years.
2. All were free of obvious organic problems (although one of the patients was diagnosed as having them).
3. All had minimal academic skills (reading, writing, and arithmetic).
4. The average age was 55.

The first three patient-assistants were chosen because of their high percentage of isolation and mutism.

Once they were trained, they helped the psychiatrist in recording behavior, maintaining an overall reliability of 78 to 87% throughout the experimental situation. After the recording behavior was well established under the point system, we extended the point contingencies to verbal communication behaviors—both cooperative and critical—of the observers as they compared their recordings. Three months after starting the program, the patient-assistants were spending three hours each day (9:30 A.M. to 12:30 P.M.) fulfilling their tasks; this represented 12.5% of their total time in the program.

In addition to the point system for the patient-assistants, we initiated a token system contingent upon certain behaviors of the other patients. This was known as the Intensive Socialization Program.

An "Intensive Socialization" workshop was available to all patients of Ward 5 from 9:30 A.M. to 12:30 P.M. daily, during which patients could participate in both academic and crafts activities. The workshop area, comprising a total area of 46 × 16.5 ft., is divided into two rooms. Those patients included in the token system received two tokens for arriving at the workshop on time (between 9:20 and 9:35 A.M.). They also received two tokens for each 20 to 30 minutes they remained in the workshop. Other tokens were earned for performance in academic tasks (reading, writing, etc.), ward upkeep, and personal appearance.

Patient-assistants were in charge of keeping track of and distributing the tokens. One of the assistants recorded in a notebook the following information for each of the patients: the number and colors of tokens earned that day for attending the workshop and for performing ward-upkeep tasks and academic tasks, as well as the number of patients who attended the workshop that day. At 11:00 A.M. he asks another patient-assistant for the day's recording of each patient's personal appearance, adding this to the other data and calculating the total number of tokens each patient was to receive. The first assistant then distributed the tokens. Finally, he asked each of the other assistants the number of points each one has earned for his respective activities and gave this information to the psychiatrist to enter on the assistants' cards.

Patients included in the token system were mainly in charge of ward upkeep and responsible for keeping the craft materials clean and in order. On the other hand, patients included in the point system were those who have developed a capacity for more delayed reinforcement. Their tasks involved recording and tabulating the data, giving out tokens, and drawing graphs. Once their daily rate had stabilized at 100 points or better, they were permitted to engage in other tasks under the heading of "Extra work." These activities included such attractive things as being permitted to paint a mural, translate writings, offer explanations to visiting psychology students, etc. Under this situation, the patients might earn high wages, that is to say, there was no limit to the points they may obtain.

The time patients participated in the fulfillment of the tasks in the program was estimated from the amount of time they spent in the "Intensive Socialization" workshop, where they had to carry out ward upkeep, record activities, and manage the contingencies. The time invested was added to the total number of workdays in a month. The same procedure was followed to estimate the percentage of participation of the psychologists in the fulfillment of the different tasks included in the program. These data are shown in Fig. 1. It is

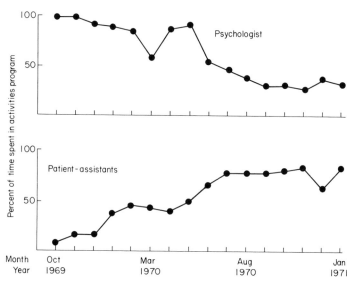

Fig. 1. Percentage of time spent in the activities of the Intensive Socialization rehabilitation program.

apparent that over the 16-month period of the study the patient-assistants were spending more time in the activities and the psychologists were spending less time in them. The "percentage of participation" as a key datum in the evaluation of group programs deserves a more thorough study than the one done here, and part of our future endeavors will be directed toward the investigation of this matter.

The various tasks carried out by the patients in the program differ in complexity (see Table 1). Advancement in the system is possible by proceeding from simple tasks to more complex ones. For example, a patient may start in the token program by merely attending the workshop and by performing the ward-upkeep tasks, which require simple motor skills. He may then move on to the more complex tasks of recording and tabulating behavior, etc., under the point program. The selection of new patient-assistants is done by the psychiatrist and three undergraduate students on the basis of the patients' previous performance. Of the 30 patients included in Ward 5's program of Intensive Socialization, there are 8 patient-assistants at present. The work of the assistants represents 80% of the total of activities carried out, while the work of the other 22 patients under the token program represents only 20%. On the other hand, the personnel conducting the research (4 persons) actually spend 38% of their time in the fulfillment of the tasks in the program.

To summarize, the problems involved in using patients as assistants are much like those encountered in the training of any other nonprofessional. Two are most apparent.

1. The problems related to the administration of the program, considering the personnel in charge.

2. The problems related to the administration and conduct of the program, considering the patient-assistants.

TABLE 1
Distribution of Activities in the Intensive Socialization Rehabilitation Program

Activities	Skills required	Program
1. Contingency management (a) Points distribution (b) Token distribution (c) Tour assistant (d) Exchange of points and tokens	Complex verbal and motor	100% points
2. Recording (a) Cleaning (b) Cooperation (c) Attendance (d) Data tabulation	Complex motor	95% points
3. Maintenance (a) Sweep and mop floors of work area (b) Clean table and chairs (c) Keep available work material	Simple motor	50% points 50% tokens

In the first set of problems, we must stress the probable exploitation of the patients by the professional personnel. As Cumming and Cumming (1957) noted, patients often turn out to be very skillful in certain tasks. This itself is not the principal goal of rehabilitation, and those in charge should not take advantage of it. One solution to this problem has been the periodic rotation of patients in the various activities (Ayllon & Azrin, 1968; Kale *et al.*, 1968). In our program, as we have said previously, rotation is carried out according to the behavioral skills displayed by the patients.

The second problem is that the patients can easily ignore or modify the decisions or criteria established by the professional personnel—modifying the availability of the reinforcers, for example. Procedures designed to deal with this problem include the introduction of a feedback system (Kale *et al.*, 1968). The mechanics of this aspect require our attention.

Our endeavors represent the first step in the process of training paraprofessionals in the role of assistants in rehabilitation programs. The total plan involves the training of both patients and undergraduate students (see the chapter by Ayllon and Wright, this volume) as well as the training of the psychologists themselves. Although our project has centered primarily on utilizing the patients as assistants, the use of undergraduates is especially promising, considering the resources of our population.

REFERENCES

Ayllon, T. Intensive treatment of psychotic behavior by stimulus satiation and food reinforcement. *Behavior Research and Therapy*, 1963, 1, 53-61.
Ayllon, T., & Azrin, N. *The token economy: A motivational system for therapy and rehabilitation.* New York: Appleton, 1968.
Ayllon, T., & Haughton, E. Control of the behavior of schizophrenic patients by food. *Journal of Experimental Analysis of Behavior*, 1962, 5, 343-352.
Ayllon, T., & Haughton, E. Modification of symptomatic verbal behavior of mental patients. *Behaviour Research & Therapy*, 1964, 2, 87-97.
Ayllon, T., & Michael, J. L. The psychiatric nurse as a behavioral engineer. *Journal of Experimental Analysis of Behavior*, 1959, 2, 323-334.
Cumming, J., & Cumming, E. Social equilibrium and social change in the large mental hospital. In M. Greenblatt, D. J. Levinson, and R. H. Williams (Eds.), *The patient and the mental hospital.* New York: Free Press, 1957.
Dominguez, T. B. Modificacion y Analisis de la conducta en pacientes mentales. *Revista Latin-America de psicologia*, 1970, 2, 123-128.
Greenblatt, M., Levinson, D. J., & Williams, R. H. (Eds.) *The patient and the mental hospital.* New York: Free Press, 1957.
Goffman, E. *Asylums. Essays on the social situation of mental patients and other inmates.* New York: Anchor Books, Doubleday, 1961.
Kale, R. J., Zlutnick, S., & Hopkins, B. L. Patient contributions to a therapeutic environment. *Michigan Mental Health Research Bulletin*, 1968, 11 (2), 33-38.
Miron, N. B. Issues and implications of operant conditioning. The primary ethical consideration. *Hospital & Community Psychiatry*, 1968, 19, 226-228.
Ulrich, R., Stachnick, T., & Mabry, J. *Control of human behavior.* Glenview, Illinois: Scott, Foresman, 1970.

An Experimental Analysis
of Clinical Phenomena[1]

C. B. FERSTER

I would like to suggest here that the contribution of behavioral therapies is complimentary rather than contradictory to insight or psychodynamic therapies. If the techniques of insight therapy modify behavior in useful ways, then they can uncover new phenomena for the behavior therapist. An objective behavioral description will then make these phenomena communicable and replicable. An objective language can contribute to psychodynamic therapies because (1) the therapist can be reinforced by small indications of progress if the component details of a long-term therapeutic interaction are readily observable; (2) experienced therapists can train others if they can accurately describe what they do; and (3) observations of the relevant component behaviors will lead to new discoveries.

The Behavior of Certain Therapists is Differentially Reinforced by the Changes that Occur in Their Patients

It is important to distinguish among several styles of clinical work to discover those therapies that are most likely to develop phenomena that are profitable to

[1] The readers' attention is directed to a paper by Michel Hersen, "The Complementary Use of Behavior Therapy and Psychotherapy: Some Comments." *Psychological Record*, 1970, 20, 395-402.
This article, in slightly modified form, is also published in the *Psychological Record*, 1972, 22, 161-167, reprinted with permission.

analyze behaviorally. Conventional clinicians, like behavior therapists, probably differ in how much their activity is planned ahead of time. For some, therapy is a prearranged protocol administered to the patient, as in a prescription; for others it is a product of the moment-to-moment interaction between them. It is the proverbial middle ground that will be the most useful. Past experience, the transmitted experience of others, and theory provide a structure that gives therapy some direction, whereas the experiential quality and the primary focus on the behavior of the individual patient constantly adapt and bend the theory and the past experience on which treatment is based. The theory suggests what to look for, but when it ceases to be useful the experienced therapist shifts to his observations of the patient's behavior and his own experience.

The changes in the patient's behavior may reinforce a therapist's behavior, even though the procedures he is using are intuitive. It is this experiential side of therapy, derived from the point-to-point interaction between patient and therapist, that leads some clinicians to describe therapy as a scientific experiment. The outcome is not known in advance, each activity is determined by the results of the previous one, and the patient teaches the therapist what is effective. The successive approximation of the therapists by the changes in behavior of the patient has potential for behavioral analysis because many of these phenomena and procedures do not appear to be discoverable in any other way. No matter how the phenomenon and methods are discovered in the first instance, however, they can become objective and communicable. If the component performances and the environmental details that control them are observed, the insight therapy may become behavioral even if it is not behavior therapy.

It is More Profitable to Analyze Clinical Practice than Clinical Theory

It is more profitable to concentrate on those parts of clinical theory and practice that suggest the underlying behavioral phenomena rather than to explain some theory in behavioral terms. The clinical terms and concepts that will be useful in uncovering new behavior are those that give evidence of the actual conduct prompting the therapist to use the terms. Terms like transference; mutative interpretation; strong, negative, or warm feelings; sense of identity; and feeling of abandonment are useful if they uncover the behavior that the clinician reacts to when he uses them. The heuristic value of the terms or the merits of the theory they represent have little relevance to a behavioral analysis. By paying attention to the behavioral observations rather than the theory, a behavioral analysis may discover kinds of conduct that are useful targets for behavior modification procedures.

BEHAVIORAL ANALYSIS OF THE ACTUAL INTERACTIONS OF DESENSITIZATION THERAPY

The dichotomy between the behavioral and insight therapeutic practices becomes less distinct when a behavioral analysis is made of the actual interaction. Despite the prescription of a scientifically based treatment plan in desensitization therapy, there are still questions on whether the stated procedures are actually the ones that produce the final result. An analysis of desensitization therapy offers one such example. Although the results of desensitization therapy are often ascribed to the extinction of conditioned aversive stimuli, other behavioral processes could contribute to the result equally.

The patient's complaint, and hence the reason for therapy, is usually nonverbal. There is difficulty with behavior in their daily lives such as going into buses, riding in elevators, handling snakes, engaging in sexual behavior, or riding a bicycle. Nevertheless, the therapeutic procedures consist almost exclusively of speech about these outside activities. Most often, the outcome of therapy is measured by the frequency of these verbal behaviors.

Increasing the Frequency of Verbal Performance by Weakening Incompatible Behavior

One important kind of behavior change that desensitization therapy may produce is a general increase in the frequency of verbal performances that are no longer suppressed by conditioned aversive reflexes. Because such suppression is not likely to be narrowly delimited, other verbal behavior will also decrease in frequency. The process, the negative reinforcement of operants incompatible with those that generate conditioned aversive stimuli, appears to be the same one that is referred to dynamically as repression. There are obvious parallels to psychoanalytic procedures in which the patient is led to talk about difficult matters paced with his ability to tolerate the discomfort that they generate.

Direct Reinforcement of Verbal Performances by the Therapist

The desensitization procedures also may teach the patient how to observe his own anxiousness. He is taught to relax sufficiently so that gross motor tensions do not mask the signs of incipient anxiousness. The patient constructs and practices exercises, with graded hierarchies of statements or thoughts that progressively provoke discomfort. These activities are the same as the formal discrimination procedures of the experimental laboratory. The performance may be raising the hand or saying, "I am anxious," and the discriminative stimulus it comes under the control of is the patient's state of anxiousness. The reinforcer is generalized. The size of the steps which the patient in the hierarchy constructs and practices depends on his ability to distinguish small increases in discomfort. Most of the events the patient learns to talk about are private.[2] Therefore the therapist requires indirect evidence of the stimuli that prompt the patient's performance. Otherwise he has no way of knowing how accurately the patient is observing his behavior.

---

[2]The term private event follows Skinner's (1957) usage. It refers to events that only one person has direct access to because they are within the skin. Usually there are public accompaniments that allow the community to reinforce discriminatively even though only one person has direct access to the event.

*The Transfer from the Therapist's Office to the Daily Events
of the Patient's Life*

The behavior changes from desensitization therapy procedures so far were mainly verbal. Suppressed verbal behavior is freed, and verbal performances are developed under the discriminative control of private events. Although the new verbal behaviors are related to the phobia that brought the patient to treatment, they are by no means identical to it. One of the most pressing questions about therapy is how procedures in an office or other limited place can have a wide effect on the patient's behavior elsewhere. Behaviorally, phobias deal with the frequency of such behaviors as walking, climbing stairs, operating elevators, or standing at bus stops. A functional analysis of how desensitization works requires discovery of a behavioral bridge between talking to a therapist in an office and a change in the frequency of standing at bus stops, putting money into a fare box, climbing the steps of a bus, etc.

The discomfort that brings the patient to therapy comes predominantly from nonverbal operant behaviors. In other words, he stays home instead of going to work, he has a reduced frequency of social contact, etc. It is unlikely, except with clinically unimportant problems, that a patient's difficulty will be limited to one kind of behavior. The fact that there is a disruption in the repertoire at all suggests that the behaviors are weak in the first place. Thus, behaviorally and clinically, a phobia is not so much a thing of itself as it is a general condition of a larger repertoire. If the baseline operant repertoire were better maintained through positive reinforcement, an aversive stimuli of a given magnitude could not disrupt it. One would not expect much help for a poorly developed overall operant repertoire from desensitization therapy alone.

Despite these conceptual difficulties, there still remains a magnitude of aversive control and a state of the overall repertoire for which desensitization therapy appears to be successful. By analyzing the patient's total repertoire, the ways that verbal behavior can influence nonverbal, or even other verbal behavior, we may discover ways of how talking in the therapist's office can influence other performances elsewhere.

The ability to react differentially and sensitively to his own behavior could provide one important basis for the bridge to the patient's natural environment. The person who can react differently and specifically to an aversive part of his natural environment that is causing anxiousness is in a position to manipulate it to reduce the aversiveness. To put the matter behaviorally, an aversive stimulus may disrupt an entire repertoire, or it can increase the frequency of some. performance that terminates it. In the classic animal experiment, the distinction is between the suppression of variable-interval food performance by a pre-aversive stimulus and an operant performance negatively reinforced by terminating the conditioned aversive stimulus. A passive person who reacts diffusely and helplessly to the unfavorable aspects of his social world is clinically parallel to the disruption of the ongoing operant repertoire by an aversive stimulus. Without a discriminative repertoire under the control of internal disruptions produced by aversive effects of the environment, it is not likely that avoidance and escape behaviors could be reinforced. The observing behaviors are critical because an aversive element of the environment could not serve as a negative reinforcer, unless some performance in the person's repertoire were under the discriminative control of the aversive stimulus. Without an ability to observe the aversive element of a complex environment there could only be either a diffuse emotional reaction or a withdrawal from the entire situation. The patient's observations of his anxiousness verbally are different, however, from his observations of the details of the environment that are producing the anxiousness. The latter requires a functional analysis of the performance as it is controlled by particular elements of the environment (usually external). Yet, the ability to notice changes in one's own internal state appears to be an important, perhaps necessary, start toward observing such a functional relation. The distinction between noticing one's own behavior and noticing the functional relation to the environment is an important one in Freudian theory, which talks about the "ability to distinguish self from not self" and ascribes to this repertoire the highest importance (Cameron, 1964). Such ability to observe and analyze the environment is, of course, a goal of most insight therapists. The term psychoanalysis, for example, more aptly describes the patient's ability to analyze his own conduct than the therapist's observation of the patient.

These observing behaviors—the tacts[3] under the control of private events—are natural events for which continued reinforcement does not depend on the arbitrary or special circumstances of the therapy situation.

THE EFFECTIVENESS OF TOKEN PROCEDURES MAY BE AN INDIRECT RESULT OF THE PROCEDURE

Token procedures in school room environments offer another example, similar to the analysis of desensitization therapy, of how a statement of clinical procedure may not account for all the reasons for its effectiveness. Even though many classroom token procedures appear to be practical and effective, it does not follow that the overall changes in the behavior of the students come only from the specific behaviors that the teacher intends to reinforce with tokens. In fact, if the control of the child's behavior by tokens and food is taken literally, it would suggest that the child would not be inclined to read elsewhere under the control of reinforcers other than food or tokens. Later, in the real world, reading will occur because of its natural consequences—the behaviors it prompts, which

---

[3] A special term, following Skinner (1957), to describe a verbal performance that is controlled by the stimulus on which occasion it is reinforced. The control by the stimulus, rather than by the reinforcer, gives the tact its objectivity, its usefulness for communication, and its common usage by different members of the community under a wide range of circumstances. In colloquial terms a tact *describes* some event. In the present case the event that the tact "describes" is within the person's skin, hence private. It is useful to talk about the tact as a verbal performance controlled by some stimulus rather than "describing" it because the former usage points to the exact procedures for establishing the behavior whereas the latter usage is mentalistic. It is for this reason that the phrase "a performance under the control of stimulus" appears frequently in this paper in place of "awareness of the stimulus" or "ability to notice the stimulus."

in turn make other behavior possible. Or, to put the matter in the reverse direction, the *inclination* to interact with the social environment by reading appears to be more crucial than the components or content of the reading behavior. Educational environments are, by definition, somewhat arbitrary, but the distinction being made is between limited discriminative control by textual stimuli, which is an element of the reading repertoire, and reading reinforced by experiences, which will sustain and enlarge the reading repertoire.

Possibly one reason for the effectiveness of token procedures is the way that they make the child's behavior more visible to the teacher as well as to the child itself. A teacher who can give a token selectively to produce specific increments in a child's behavior is also becoming more observant and, hence, more sensitive to other aspects of the child's repertoire. Under these conditions, not only will she give tokens but she will also attend to the child selectively and differentially, she will prompt other behaviors related to the target of the token procedures, and she will react to components of long-range programs that make detailed and intimate contact with the individual aspects of the child's behavior. She will also be able to observe the child's immediate concerns and, hence, react more effectively to the child's immediate repertoire.

On the child's part, the token amplifies the product of his conduct so that he can observe his progress and competence. The child's increased ability to see his own progress and hence be reinforced by it is as much a product of a new classroom structure as it is a result of direct reinforcement of behavior by the token itself. The teacher who individualizes instruction in her classroom soon creates a totally new environment in which her role shifts to an advisory, programming, and reactive role in which she designs tasks clearly within the child's competence and builds a total classroom environment that shifts with these changes after they occur.

THE PROCEDURES OF INSIGHT THERAPY

The actual behavioral processes underlying the procedures and practices of insight therapy are no more obvious than those underlying desensitization therapy. Even though insight therapists frequently use mentalistic language, such as talking about the patient's feelings and rejecting the patient's emitted behavior as a surface manifestation of an inner problem, it is usually possible to know many of the behavioral circumstances that prompt clinical descriptions. Mentalistic terms, like feelings and emotional tone, which put the locus of action inside the patient, appear to be designed to resolve the discrepancy between the overt form of the patient's behavior and its function. In other cases, the patient's internal state of feelings is invoked to describe the frequency or strength of the behavior—strong feelings are generally equivalent to a high frequency of behavior. The clinical use of the term feelings is an extension of ordinary speech, as for example, "I feel very strongly that. . . ." Behaviorally this describes the repertoire of a person who will sustain behavior reinforced by its persuasive effect on others. "He doesn't express his feelings" usually describes a repertoire where certain behaviors are not being emitted despite collateral evidence that would lead an observer to expect a higher frequency. An interpretation of a patient's feelings, such as "You seem to feel angry," is usually a functional analysis that summarizes very different forms of behavior by indicating that they are controlled by a single variable—the aversive effect they generate on someone's behavior. The performances range from a funny story at someone's expense, a high frequency of reporting unfavorable events, facial expressions, mispronouncing a name, to direct criticism. These are angry feelings clinically; behaviorally they are a potentially high frequency of performances that present aversive stimuli to others; or they are generated by an unfavorable event like an insult, a loss of property, or a withdrawal of attention or affection. The performances that lead the clinician to infer a common controlling variable are mostly directly observable in the immediate therapeutic situation and, hence, potentially as available to the patient as to the therapist.

Insight Therapies Emphasize the Development of Self-Observation

Much of insight therapy appears to be directed toward the development of self-observation. Functionally, the therapist's verbal reactivity reinforces behavior that describes (is under the discriminative control of) other verbal behavior. When a patient says, "I wanted to stay longer, but I left anyway," the therapist is likely to reply, "Tell me more about it." The persistent reinforcement of behavior that describes behavior is designed to generate a repertoire of self-observation or awareness, including a description of the functional significance of the patient's behavior. The importance of self-awareness and self-observation is at the heart of psychodynamic theory. Primary narcissism, for example, represents the minimal amount of self-observation and awareness. Normal growth and development consists of an increased control of the child's behavior by the characteristics of the environment reinforcing it. Behaviorally, primary narcissism refers to a repertoire of the emitted operant behavior without any accommodation to the characteristics of the environment that can potentially support it. The failure to observe and accommodate to the characteristics of the external environment is a deficiency in repertoire that will obviously prevent both the avoidance of aversive elements and the development of an effective interaction with the full complexity of the normal environment.

Behaviorally, a person learns to observe when a performance comes under the control of a stimulus. The shift in language from "perceiving or observing a stimulus" to "a performance under the control of a stimulus" allows a behavioral rather than a mentalistic description. A description of the control of a performance by a stimulus has an advantage over an introspective account, because it reveals the actual behaviors that the patient and therapist are reacting to and their functional relation to the objective features of the environment.

The Kinds of Self-Observation That Are Difficult

It is difficult to teach a patient to observe his own behavior because so much of it is private or of such a small public magnitude that it is essentially covert.

Three kinds of events that need to be observed are the person's physiological and somatic state, the strength of latent behavior in the repertoire, and the functional relation between the performance and the element of the environment that controls it. Clinical descriptions do not always differentiate among these different kinds of events. When a patient says he is angry, the discriminative stimulus controlling this verbal performance may be a physiological one—or the disruptive effect of physiological changes on the ongoing repertoire—or it could be an increased frequency of aggresive behaviors. Often the patient can describe the internal physiological state but lacks verbal behavior about the events in the outside environment that generate it. Other patients may be able to describe neither the external events nor the changes they elicit within his skin. Others, able to describe an increased frequency of actual or latent operant behavior, are unable to describe it functionally in relation to the environment controlling it.

Skinner's (1953; 1957) discussion of verbal behavior under the discriminative control of private events applies directly to the problem of defects of self-awareness. The development of these behaviors in therapy appears to be almost the same as in normal growth and development. The child learns to describe his physiological state, his incipient or latent behavior, and the functional significance of his behavior in response to questions like "How do you feel?", "Where are you going?", or "Why did you do it?"

Probably the most significant and difficult event to learn to observe is the functional relation between one's own behavior and the element of the environment that controls it. In general, a factual account of what happened is not nearly as useful as the relation between the events and the part of the environment that controls them. When a child who hears that someone is sick says, "I hope he won't die," we cannot know whether the performance should be classified as avoidance or punishment. The performance is avoidance of the loss of positive reinforcement if the child is apprehensive about the possibility of death. It is punishment if it is a performance reinforced by the injury it produces—if he is angry at the person. It is particularly difficult to observe the functional significance of behavior when the performances are distorted by multiple contingencies, particularly punishment. In these cases, very strong behavior may be observed only indirectly because only indirect forms are emitted. Clinical descriptions summarize apparently different, but functionally similar events as a statement of the patient's feelings or as the emotional tone of the acts. Behaviorally, they are performances with different topographies that alter the environment in the same way. In both cases the theoretical description serves to differentiate between performances that are topographically different but functionally similar. When clinicians assert that behavioral descriptions are insufficient, they are speaking of the necessity of a functional analysis. Behavioral language, however, has the advantage of describing events in the outside environment about which consensus is easy rather than an internal state, which needs to be inferred indirectly.

Interpretation

Interpretation, which is such a prominent feature of most insight therapies, is given such importance because so many patients are unable to observe more than the topography or content of their behavior. Traditionally, the "insight" therapist interprets the patient's feelings; that is, he tells the patient the functional analysis he has made of the behavior they observe together during therapy. Whatever other significance interpretations may have in various clinical theories, behaviorally they are *tacts* under the control of the patient's behavior. In more common language, they are verbal behavior that describes the patient's verbal behavior. A behavioral account of what happens when a clinician makes an interpretation requires an analysis of the verbal interaction between therapist and patient as speaker and listener when they maintain and alter the frequency of each other's behavior.

Interpretations are difficult technically because the clinician cannot simply tell the patient what his repertoire is and what is controlling it. If he did so the resulting verbal behaviors would be *intraverbal*, like memorizing poetry. Whether the patient learns how to describe his own conduct, with some instruction from the therapist, or whether he is emitting behavior reinforced by the attention and differential reactivity of the therapist is a subtle distinction of crucial importance from a behavioral as well as from a clinical point of view. The distinction is between the direct reinforcement of verbal behavior by the therapist and a verbal performance under the control of a stimulus by differential reinforcement. In common language, we ask whether the patient has observed an event directly or whether he is saying the kinds of things that could have been discovered by observing the event. The problem is doubly difficult because the verbal performances are topographically identical in the two cases.

The Reinforcement of Observing Behavior

Verbal behaviors that occur because they are reinforced by the therapist are arbitrary because they are narrowly controlled by the therapist and, hence, potentially unavailable to the patient in the absence of the therapist's special purposes. The therapist contributes by providing an opportunity to make the patient's observation more visible, more overt, and more frequent. In such a case, however, the primary control is by the events in the patient's life rather than the reaction of the therapist. The distinction is between natural and arbitrary reinforcement of the patient's verbal performances (Ferster, 1967). In the arbitrary case, the patient's verbal performances are observations in only a limited and literal sense. Technically, they are impure tacts[4] (according to

---

[4] An impure tact is a verbal performance for which control is shared by the stimulus that prompts it and a reinforcer relevant to the speaker's current level of deprivation. If the tact were pure, its form would be controlled solely by the stimulus to the exclusion of any reinforcers relevant to the speaker's current state of deprivations.

Skinner's usage of the term) because they are reinforced by the therapist rather than by a generalized reinforcer. For example, the therapist may react especially to comments about sexual behavior or to some other performance that fits into a preconceived treatment plan. In the natural case, the reinforcer maintaining the verbal observation is reinforced because it clarifies the environment by providing discriminative stimuli for the reinforcement of other behaviors. The role of the therapist is that of an audience rather than a reinforcer; he reacts only to self-observation, leaving the form and content of the observation to depend on the patient's dispositions. Even when the therapist may selectively encourage the patient to note those behaviors that give evidence of the highest potential frequency, the content of the patient's observations will be a product of his unique history of reinforcement rather than of direct reinforcement by the therapist.

Timing

At the heart of clinical interpretation is its timing. The ability to influence a group or an individual by commenting or observing depends less on the correctness or importance of the observation than whether it can prompt an increase in the frequency of behaviors already prominent in the patient's repertoire. In technical language, the effectiveness of an interpretation will depend on whether the functional description of the patient's behavior is a discriminative stimulus, a tact, under the control of events in his own life, or intraverbals,[5] reinforced by the therapist, like memorizing facts. The delicacy of an effectively timed interpretation is reminiscent of Goethe's advice that you can only teach a student what he already knows.

From a behavioral analysis, many successful changes in the patient's behavior need to occur before there is a substantial enough repertoire that exists in a high enough frequency to be prompted by an interpretation. In fact, psychotherapy may be thought of as a series of procedures to develop new repertoires that cumulate in successful interpretations. As a minimum, the patient needs to emit a high enough frequency of verbal behavior so that it can be differentially reinforced.

The patient's lifelong habitual patterns of action provide one kind of behavior that can be observed and analyzed in the immediate therapy situation, because the therapist's neutral position provides a setting in which the patient's characteristic manner of action can be enacted. This, of course, is the behavior that is clinically called transference.

Performances reinforced directly by the reactivity of the therapist are still another source of behavior for observation and analysis in the therapy environment. The therapy situation is a stable interaction in which two people reinforce, shape, and sustain each other's behavior. The gross behavioral events in

---

[5] A verbal performance under the control of a previous verbal performance as in a chain of behaviors. "Quick as a wink" is an example of an intraverbal sequence of performances. There is little point-to-point correspondence between each of the words in the sequence and a corresponding effect on the listener.

the immediate therapeutic situation therefore provide an opportunity for interpretation and description because they are an approximation to the kinds of observations that can be made elsewhere. The patient's speech "to the therapist" has two simultaneous functions. First, it is a tact, usually quite distorted and impure, under the control of the childhood event (or any other past event the patient is talking about) or perhaps even some intraverbal residue of the past event. More important, however, it is a performance whose form has been shaped by speakers whom the patient has influenced in the past. If the latent reactivity of the therapist is similar to those individuals who have maintained the patient's behavior in the past, the verbal episode will be successful and stable. To the extent that the therapist does not react in the same way as the patient's past listeners have, there is an opportunity, first, for differential reinforcement, and second, for observation of the discrepancy between the patient's behavior and reinforcement by the therapist.

The significance of the therapist's reinforcement of the patient's speech is in the functional relation between the two repertoires rather than the specific content of what the patient is saying. When a patient is telling a therapist, for example, about his childhood, the effect that is generated in the therapist, as a listener, is a more important characteristic of his verbal behavior than the event which it describes. The reinforcer, in such a verbal episode, is a subtle one, at the heart of the definition of verbal reinforcement.[6] The delicate interaction between two people that occurs when someone tries to explain something illustrates the process. There is give and take as the speaker and listener play on each other until the listener says he understands and the speaker is no longer inclined to explain because the listener can now say what he was trying to explain. Functionally, the patient's speech is primarily a performance reinforced by "making the therapist understand" and only secondarily a performance describing the patient's past life. The advantage of such a functional relation between therapist and patient, listener and speaker, is that the interaction reinforces (hence increases the frequency) of explanations and observation of the patient's life. The therapist's ability to make a functional analysis of the emitted behavior he is observing in the immediate situation and his interest in the patient's observations gives a unique advantage to his verbal reactivity.

A Successful Interpretation

One criteria of success of an interpretation is whether it prompts a verbal performance in the patient's repertoire, under the discriminative control of his own behavior, which has the same essential elements that are prompted in the repertoire of the therapist when he is observing the same events. The observations remain the patient's, but the particular dimension that exerts special control may be a product of the therapist's rephrasing, suggestion, or question (prompt). The ultimate validation of an interpretation is, of course, a behavioral change beyond the immediate conversation.

[6]For an elaboration of the definition of verbal reinforcement see Skinner (1957), pp. 224-225.

Group therapy provides useful examples of interpretation, because the group's task is to analyze its immediate behavior—the interactions among the members and between the members and leaders. A common occurrence in therapy groups is a long and uncomfortable silence, which occurs because the performance that has the highest potential frequency cannot occur for some reason. The therapist, for example, observes a slow and depressed conversation from which he draws the conclusion that the group as a whole is sad because the sessions are going to end in two weeks. He judges that the behaviors he has observed, as well as their covert counterparts, are visible enough to the group members that he can attempt to prompt observations of them. When he comments that everyone seems sad and wonders whether the end of the meetings was the reason, the conversation increases in frequency. Someone remarks that they will miss the group meetings, another says how much benefit there was, and another indicates some remaining items of business for which there is still time to deal with. Sometimes the therapist's interpretation will be prompted by remarks about difficult personal losses and separations, which members of the group have encountered in their past lives. In that event, the interpretation may be a comment linking the past losses experienced by the patient with the threat of loss currently experienced in the therapy group. The force of this interpretation in this case is to prompt (hence increase the frequency) of two related performances simultaneously so that the patient can observe them together. The final observation is one performance controlled by the two events.

Circumstances surrounding a group's evasion of its task are often interpreted. An anxiety-provoking event may often lead a group to "chit chat," an atmosphere suggestive of a cocktail party. For example, a member of the group who had been roundly criticized the previous time fails to appear. If the therapists indeed have evidence that the light conversation is avoidance behavior negatively reinforced because it is prepotent over discussions of the missing member and the worry about the extent of their responsibility for his absence, he might describe the group's current behavior and ask whether it is being produced by concern over the missing group member. A comment to this effect may suddenly change the atmosphere to a gloomy depressed silence from which a discussion slowly emerges about whether someone's unkind treatment was responsible for the missing member's absence. When the circumstances surrounding the absence are sufficiently clear, the conversation shifts to a new topic without interference by high frequency behavior that cannot be emitted. A therapist may speak only several times an hour, but if the remarks are successful interpretations, they produce dramatic alterations in the frequency of the group's behavior.

If the interpretation and its timing is correct, the frequency of observing the troublesome event (controlling the behavior that could not be emitted) increases. The overt occurrence of verbal performances, under the specific control of the disruptive aversive event, clarifies the control of their behavior for the group. The unanalyzed environment disrupts the group's behavior because an aversive stimulus controls a performance that has a latent frequency of occurrence higher than any other available behaviors. Their prepotency over other performances prevent any other activity. When these high frequency, latent behaviors can be emitted and, hence, act on the environment to alter the conditions that generated them originally, the group can turn to other matters. When the members of the group can observe how the impending dissolution of the group or the circumstances surrounding the group member's absence influenced them, specific behaviors under the control of the aversive elements by negative reinforcement can reduce the aversiveness that had been so disruptive. The distinction is the same as that between the disruptive effect of a preaversive stimulus and the negatively reinforced operants generated by its removal or diminution.

TRANSFERENCE

No account of insight therapy would be complete without a discussion of transference because so many of the patient's behaviors with which the therapist interacts come from styles of conduct that have been recurrent and characteristic during the patient's lifetime. The behavior inappropriate to his environment, which brought the patient to therapy, is also likely to be inappropriate for his interaction with the therapist. These are performances that do not effectively alter the patient's environment in ways that are important to him or that produce a harmful result. The performances can be characterized by the fact that they are inappropriate to the variable that generates them. For example, the patient reacts as if an acquaintance is bullying him when, in fact, the acquaintance is very positive. Another patient gets angry because his friend does not anticipate one of his wishes. It would be as if the food-deprived rat, in an environment in which pressing the lever produces a food pellet, should emit a high and persistent frequency of staring at the lever from the distant corner of the cage. In all of these cases, the variable generating the behavior remains unaffected even after the performance occurs. In psychodynamic terms, there has been no release in tension.

Since most of the behaviors for which therapy is required concern performances reinforced socially, that is, by their influence on another person, the personal reactivity of the therapist provides a model situation in which many of the inappropriate behavioral interactions between the patient and various people he deals with frequently can occur. The neutrality of the therapist is vitally important if the patient is to be in a position to observe the mismatch between his conduct and the potential reactivity of the current environment. Though the therapist's neutrality does not exclude reinforcement of the patient's behavior, the behaviors that are reinforced are the observation of what is occurring rather than conforming to the demand[7] the patient places on the therapist. Group therapy is a useful place to observe transference behaviors because the therapeutic procedure emphasizes the current behavior of the group members as they deal with each other and with the therapist. Groups consistently begin by

---

[7]Technically, a mand (Skinner, 1957, Chapter 3).

looking to the therapist to tell them what to do, to provide a cure for their difficulties, and to explain what is wrong. Instead, the therapist observes carefully, describes to the group members what is happening, and interacts selectively to their current behavior.

In the group's early stages, the members tend to sit passively and wait for the leader to tell them what to do. The classic response to this opening circumstance is for the group leader to ask whether everyone is sitting in silence because they are expecting the therapist to take the lead and proceed with some kind of therapeutic procedures to which the group will react passively. This inevitably leads to a discussion of what the group members expect from their group interaction (and the therapist). Questions directed to the therapist tend to be deflected with comments that shift the group's attention back to analyzing the circumstances that led the group or the group members to ask direct advice. Some times the therapist's comment will be an observation of some of the immediate circumstances surrounding the remark. Other times his answer may be evasive and nonresponsive such as, "I think the reason for your needing assurance from me about this matter is probably more important than the particular answer I could give you or the assurances I could give." Such a remark is functionally equivalent to the differential reinforcement of other behavior because it specifies a class of behavior (direct demands on the therapist) that will not be reinforced. Almost any other kind of behavior can be reinforced in some way. Members of a therapy group commonly become angry at the therapist during the first group meetings. The therapist, of course, resists pressure for a prescriptive cure, or a "laying on of hands," simply by not complying. Instead, observations of the group members' evasion of the task of self analysis is described and interpreted. "You wish we could prescribe a cure that will solve your problems," for example. In the meantime, in the course of searching about for a way to get the therapist to "produce a cure," the members of the group join forces, manipulate each other, and otherwise reinforce each other's behavior to evade difficult work to find comfort or to pressure the therapist. All of this, the therapist continues to describe. Thus, as a by-product of the therapist's neutrality, the intergroup performances, usually called the group process, increase in frequency, are interpreted by the therapist, and are reinforced by the group members. Concurrently, performances for which possible reinforcement comes from the demand they place on the therapist decrease in frequency. The term transference appears to derive from the history of reinforcement originally responsible for the performances. The therapist's neutrality guarantees that there is no current reinforcer for such behavior. When the primitive demands for a cure by the therapist decrease in frequency enough that the group members interact with each other and observe and interpret their interaction, one of the substantial goals of the therapy has been achieved.

ACKNOWLEDGMENT

I wish to thank John L. Cameron for making helpful suggestions when he read an earlier draft of this chapter.

REFERENCES

Cameron, J. L. Lectures to the Washington, D.C. Psychoanalytic Society on Ego Psychology, 1964.

Ferster, C. B. Arbitrary and natural reinforcement. *Psychological Record*, 1967, **17**, 341-347.

Skinner, B. F. *Science and human behavior.* New York: Macmillan, 1953.

Skinner, B. F. *Verbal behavior.* New York: Appleton, 1957.

Author Index

Numbers in italics refer to the pages on which the complete references are listed.

A

Akers, R. L., 88, *91*

Allen, K. E., 39 *42*, 43, *49*, 117, 118, *122*, *123*, *125*

Alper, T. A., 16, *17*

Armstrong, M., 117, 118, 124

Arnold C. R., 100, *107*, 120, *121*, *123*

Ault, M. H. A., 10, *17*, 29, 38, *42*, 43, *49*

Ayllon, T., 20, *24*, 47, *48*, 87, *91*, 116, 117 119, *123*, 128, 132, *132*

Azrin, N., 47, *48*, 87, *91*, 117, *123*, 128 132, *132*

B

Baer, D. M., 9, 13, 15, *17*, *18*, 22, *24*, 43, 45, *48*, *49*, 117, 118, 120, 121, *122*, *123*, *124*

Bailey, J. S., 55, *62*, 105, *107*

Baker, B. L., 117, 118, 119, 120, *125*

Baldwin, A. L., 38, *41*

Bandura, A., 8, *17*

Barberich, J. P., 45, *49*

Barker, R. G., 8, *17*, 38, *41*

Barrett, B. H., 118, *123*

Becker, W. C., 11, 13, *17*, *18*, 100, *107*, 117, 118, 120, 121, *123*, *124*, *125* 111, 113

Bijou, S. W., 9, 10, 13, *17*, *18*, 22, *24*, 28, 29, 31, 32, 34, 38, 39, 40, *41*, *42*, 43, 45, 48, *48*, *49*, 118, 120, 121, *123*

Birnbrauer, J. S., 28, 31, 32, *42*

Bis, J. S., 47, *49*, 65, *83*

Blattner, J. E., 118, *124*

Boozer, H., 22, *25*, 117, 120, *124*

Brawley, E. R., 117, 118, *123*

Breese, F. H., 38, *41*

Broden, M., 117, 120, 121, *123*

Brodsky, G., 16, *17*

Bronfenbrenner, U., 105, *107*

Brown, G. D., 117, *125*

Brown, P., 117, 119, *123*

Buehler, R. E., 11, *17*

Buell, J. S., 15, *17*, 118, *123*

Burchard, J. D., 47, *49*, 87, *91*, 117, *123*

Burgess, R. L., 88, *91*

Burke, M., 39, *42*

Bushell, D., Jr., 117, 118, 121, *123*, *124*

Butterfield, W. H., 100, *107*

C

Caldwell, B., 34, *42*

Cameron, J. L., 137, *147*

Cantrell, R. M., 48, *49*

Cantrell, R. P., 48, *49*

Cloward, R. D., 101, *107*

Cobb, J. A., 14, 15, *18*, 22, *25*

Cohn, A., 57, *62*

Cohen, H. L., 47, *49*, 63, 64, 65, 66, 67, 83, 84

Cole, R., 23, *25*

Conderman, L., 117, 120, 121, *124*

Cooper, B. R., 117, 119, 120, 121, *125*

Cormier, W. H., 10, *18*

Cowles, J. T., 2, *6*

Cox, M. A., 29, 39, *42*

Crosson, J. E., 47, *49*

Cummings, E., 132, *132*

Cummings, J., 132, *132*

Curtis, K. A., 10, *18*

D

Davison, G. C., 117, 118, 119, 120, 121, *123*

DeBaca, P., 22, *24*

DeSouza e Silva, S., 23, 24, *25*

Dominguez, T. B., 127, *132*

Duncan, D. F., 11, *17*

Dunn, L. M., 34, *42*

E

Ebner, M., 16, *17*

Elliott, R., 117, 119, *123*

Subject Index

A

Academic behavior, precurrent, 36
    techniques of modifying, 36
Achievement Place, 54
    behavior modification system, 54
    modifying classroom behavior, 54-57
    semi-self-governing system. 58-61
    training program for parents, 57
Anti-social behavior, 66
    difficulties in elimination, 66
Assessment, 8
    and treatment, 8
    techniques, child, 11
    techniques, child, 34
Attending behavior, 112
    in nursery school children, 112
Aversive controls, 64-65, *see also* pun-
        ishment
    limits, 64-65

B

Behavioral measures, 86
    versus standardized measures, 86-87
Behavioral repertoire, 21
    deviant child, 21
Behavior modification, 4
    and applied research, 4-5
    and decision making, 5-6
    and environmental modification, 5
    and rehabilitation problems, 47
    problems, technical, 9
    techniques easily taught, 116
Behavior program, *see also* behavior modi-
        fication
    extensions of, 111
    generalization of behavior, 111

C

Changes in patients' behavior, 133
    as reinforcers for therapists, 133-134
Classroom behavior, *see also* assessment
    monitoring techniques, 37

Clinical interpretation, 142
    timing, significance of, 142
Clinical theory, 134
    and clinical practice, 134
Crime, 66
    causes, 66

D

Delinquency program, 90
    demonstration versus service, 90-91
    strategies, 91
Delinquent behavior, 88
    determinants, 88-89
    in Latin America, 90-91
Deviant behavior, 10
    assessment of, 10, 20-21
    maintenance of, 21
    prevention of, 23-24
    stimulus settings for, 9-10
    treatment tactics, 12-13
    treatment techniques, 21-23
Direct intervention, *see also* behavior
        program and intensive socializa-
        tion program
    prosthetic environment, 89-90
Direct observation, 10
    as assessment technique, 10, 34

E

Education, 6
    current condition, 6
    hierarchical process, 113
Emitted and elicited behavior, *see* oper-
        ant and respondent conditioning
Environments, prosthetic, 87
    follow-up studies, 87-88
    generalization of the effects, 87-88
    versus direct intervention, 89-90
Experimental analysis of behavior, 5
    contribution, 5
    definition, 6
    history of, 4